YOUR LIFE ON PURPOSE

how to find what matters
& create the life you want

WITHDRAWN

Matthew McKay, Ph.D.

John P. Forsyth, Ph.D.

Georg H. Eifert, Ph.D.

New Harbinger Publications, Inc.

Publisher's Note

This publication is designed to provide accurate and authoritative information in regard to the subject matter covered. It is sold with the understanding that the publisher is not engaged in rendering psychological, financial, legal, or other professional services. If expert assistance or counseling is needed, the services of a competent professional should be sought.

Distributed in Canada by Raincoast Books

Copyright © 2010 by Matthew McKay, John P. Forsyth, and Georg H. Eifert
New Harbinger Publications, Inc.
5674 Shattuck Avenue
Oakland, CA 94609
www.newharbinger.com

Acquired by Catharine Sutker; Cover design by Amy Shoup;
Text design by Michele Waters-Kermes; Edited by Jasmine Star

Library of Congress Cataloging-in-Publication Data

McKay, Matthew.
  Your life on purpose : how to find what matters and create the life you want / Matthew McKay, John P. Forsyth, and Georg H. Eifert.
    p. cm.
  ISBN 978-1-57224-905-9 (printed book) -- ISBN 978-1-57224-907-3 (pdf ebook)
  1. Self-realization. 2. Acceptance and commitment therapy. 3. Conduct of life. I. Forsyth, John P. II. Eifert, Georg H., 1952- III. Title.
  BF637.S4M26 2010
  170'.44--dc22

                    2010028473

FSC
Mixed Sources
Product group from well-managed forests and other controlled sources
Cert no. SW-COC-002283
www.fsc.org
© 1996 Forest Stewardship Council

12 11 10   10 9 8 7 6 5 4 3 2 1   First printing

For Jordan. I'll see you, sweet boy.

—MM

For my kids, Claire, Aidan, and Maggie, and all the children in this world who dream of a better tomorrow. You are the new day. Make it shine. Everything you do, everything you've been given, has a purpose. You have a purpose too. Make your life be about something greater than yourself. Give it your all. Leave no regrets. Defend your values tenaciously and share easily. Be willing to make mistakes. Be generous with your time. And live every moment as if it were your last. Above all, cherish the bonds you have and those you create. For in those bonds, you will find your enduring legacy— a legacy built on your unlimited capacity to share faith, love, kindness, and compassion.

—JPF

This is for my sons, Daniel and Leonardo. For your own sake, I hope you won't waste your lives and opportunities by being idle or by chasing meaningless tokens or "feeling good" without engaging in purpose-driven action. Instead, listen to your heart and listen carefully. Then follow your dreams and be persistent. Use what you've got and give it your very best shot. Glimpses of happiness and feelings of contentment will follow from the pursuit of your dreams, and without ever having to chase those feelings. Even when you're young, your time on this planet is limited—use it wisely, so that in the end you can say, "No regrets."

—GHE

Contents

Acknowledgments

This book was born out of our three lives and some painful struggles. It was born out of shared wisdom, sweat, and tears. And it was born out of both hardship and pain, joys and triumphs, our own and those of others. This is important to understand. None of this was easy, and in fact, this book was born amidst incredible pain—none of it of our own choosing.

On the eve of writing this book, a twenty-something was on his thousand-dollar bike, headed for home after visiting a dear friend. He was a smart and gentle soul, with great potential and dreams of working in the film industry. About two blocks from his apartment, in a sleepy neighborhood, a shot rang out. He fell to the ground, and with his last breath dragged himself to the nearest doorstep for help. It was too late. His bike and backpack remained on the street, a car sped off into the night, and this boy never saw the dawning of the new day. A life snuffed out by unnamed thugs, a future snatched in an instant—that was one of our sons.

As we wrote this book, one of our moms and her husband were just entering their retirement years. They had worked hard all of their lives and had sacrificed their own interests and desires for the benefit of the family. That's just the kind of people they were: rich in faith and generosity. They delayed many things, thinking that retirement would be the time to live their dreams. But that dream was soon dashed. A mother's routine trip to fetch the laundry in the basement turned into a desperate cry to her husband: "I can't get upstairs. I can't feel my legs. Call 911!"

She was in good health until then, but within a span of weeks things changed. No longer sleeping with her husband, she was confined to the first floor, in a rented hospital bed in the living room. After months of tests with the best doctors, her diagnosis remained unknown. That's still true today. Her legs are swollen, and the pain is constant. She can no longer feel her bladder and bowels. So now she's connected to a catheter, wears a diaper, and relies on a walker to get around. Her mind has remained sharp, but physically she cannot do the things she had hoped to do during her retirement, like travel to see the world and visit her sixteen grandchildren and her three sons and daughters-in-law. As we were finishing this book, she told her husband, "Life is short." She's right.

And as we wrote this book, our hearts were torn apart with concern over our children, our lifeblood. Two of us watched a son and a daughter slip in and out of addictions, one with drugs and alcohol, and the other with food and weight, just dying to be thin. We dropped many things and spent hours in rehab, outpatient therapy, and counseling. We were desperate to save our children from a life of misery, or even from death. Each painful moment became an opportunity for us to grow or retreat. Each painful moment brought us back to what really matters, our values as parents, when it could have sent us adrift.

These were some of our darkest hours, a roller coaster ride of enticing, short-lived moments of hope and wellness offset by backslides into old and familiar self-destructive behaviors. These are secretive forms of suffering. One never knows if it's all finally in the past. That's the lurking fear—a fear that we dealt with while writing this book and one we will probably have to carry with us for many years to come.

And each of us had a great deal of support along the way. We are grateful to our wives and families, who stood by us during our shared trials—and through the long hours and late-night writing binges. They believed in us and the value of this book, even when it may have seemed that we stuck in a funk, adrift and confused, and wondering what it all means and whether anything really matters. They were there in our mind's eye during every keystroke, every edit, each long hour we spent holed up in our thoughts and the world of ideas and expression. None of that was easy for us or for them.

We are also grateful for the wonderful support and encouragement of our friends at New Harbinger. We'd especially like to thank Catharine Sutker, for believing in the message of this book and standing with us as we worked hard to get it right, and even as we missed deadlines to get it right. We'd also like to thank senior editor Jess Beebe for shepherding us through early drafts of the book. We also owe a debt of gratitude to Jasmine Star, for treating us with her masterful editing and kind advice. We couldn't have done it without you, Jasmine.

We'd also like to acknowledge that many of the ideas in this book are not ours to claim. In fact, much of what we share with you has been informed by a growing group of individuals working to develop a psychological science that is more adequate to the human condition. This effort does not disavow the pain and hardship of life. Instead, it offers people a way to go forward with their hurts and trials *and* create a life of meaning, purpose, dignity, and wholeness—a life worth living. You'll find this work reflected in a new evidence-based approach known as acceptance and commitment therapy (or ACT, said as one word). To be clear, this book is not about a specific type of therapy. It's a book on how to create a life that matters. ACT is an approach that's very much about how to do that, and with a growing scientific community to back it up.

We'd also like to thank all of the people who have cared enough to share their trials and tribulations, hopes and dreams, struggles and joys, hardships and pains. We've been touched and profoundly influenced by the pebbles they've dropped and the ripples they've created in our lives. We're stronger and wiser for it. You'll hear our voice and theirs as you read on.

Finally, we want to thank you for taking the time to risk reading this book. Living a life on purpose is probably one of the most difficult things you'll ever do. And this book was one of the hardest ones we've ever written. It's hard because there's a lot at stake here. Each of us gets to travel this path only once, but if we work it right, once is enough.

We hope that you find something in this book to help you make the most of your one precious life. Make it matter. Make it be about something. That's the greatest gift you can give yourself and those you touch on your journey. Do it while you can!

Peace, Love, and Life!
John, Matthew, and Georg

Chapter 1

It's Your Life:
If Not Now, When?

Our souls are hungry for meaning, for the sense that we have figured out how to live so that our lives matter... What frustrates us and robs our lives of joy is this absence of meaning... Does our being alive matter?

—Harold S. Kushner

It is only when we truly know and understand that we have a limited time on earth and that we have no way of knowing when our time is up that we will begin to live each day to the fullest, as if it were the only one we had.

—Elisabeth Kübler Ross

Time is the coin of your life. It is the only coin you have, and only you can determine how it will be spent. Be careful lest you let other people spend it for you.

—Carl Sandburg

Life is a journey. Your journey began at the moment you were born and will continue for as long as you're alive. You had no choice in starting it, but you do have a voice in what you do with the time you've been given. Whether your life is one of happenstance or clear purpose and direction pivots on knowing what kind of journey you'd like to take. You need something to guide you, an inner sense of knowing what really matters to you. This book was written to help you have that before it's too late. If you're willing, then we invite you to start by considering three questions.

What is the purpose of life?

What is the purpose of my life?

Am I living my life on purpose?

Just about everyone has considered these questions at least once. People differ in how they answer the first two, and like discussions of politics or religion, they tend to spark lively conversation and debate.

The third question, though, is different. There's no escaping the answer. You're a living and breathing testament about whether it's true for you. But you need to know what you're living for in order to answer it; only then can you see if you're on the right track. So do you know what really matters most in your life? Do you really know? And are you living a life that matters on purpose? If not, it's time to wake up.

This is your life. Nobody else can live it for you. And it matters that you live it because you're living it anyway. How you live your life impacts you, and also many, many other people. This is important to understand. You can approach your life as if your purpose is just to get by until the clock runs out, or you can work to make something of every moment you have. There are really only two ways to go here. Both are choices. Only you can make the choice to live your life on purpose. Will you?

Life is short, and it's hard—yet it can be good, too. However you see it, you have only a finite amount of time on this planet. If you live in an industrialized country, you've got about seventy-eight years, or 28,489 days. That's the average. And one-third of this time you will spend asleep—that's right, one-third.

So what you have to work with in terms of living time is more like 18,992 days. And depending on how old you are now, you've already taken a sizable bite out of the waking time you've been allotted. This waking time is important, because this is where you can act to make a difference in your life.

Time will march on, like it or not. The most important question is how will you use it? People come to this question, and to a book such as this, with different motivations. Some are suffering. Some are longing. Some are looking for growth. Others are wallowing and feeling stuck. Some are curious. Others are content and simply seek to affirm that they're on the right track. Some fear and worry. They fear that in looking at what matters they'll face the precipice between life and death and be overwhelmed by the weight of lost time and the burden of missed opportunities and regrets.

Many also worry about what tomorrow will bring for them and for those they love. Will they fall, and if so, how far? And many more come to this place not knowing what path to take. They're lost and searching for a sense of purpose, meaning, and direction. They're looking for a compass that will help guide them through difficulty and pain and toward opportunities, joys, and wholeness. What are your motivations for picking up this book?

Motivations for the Journey

Before getting into the heart of the journey we're about to take you on, we'd like to share a few stories. These stories are about people just like you. They arrived at this place, this moment in time, for a reason. They couldn't put a finger on it at first, but they knew in their gut and heart that something was amiss in how they were living their lives. Each story captures different motivations, and all reflect aspects of the human condition. See if any of these stories resonate with you and your life up until now.

Meaningless Tokens

Just about everyone will come to a point when they pause to consider how they've been living their life. Steven, a forty-three-year-old entrepreneur, arrived at this moment almost by accident. He was living the good life by most standards. He had his health, a nice home, a loving marriage, two cars, a dog, and a baby girl.

Steven also greatly enjoyed his work, so much so that he spent countless hours at the office writing, creating, and problem solving. And when he wasn't doing that, he was traveling and networking with colleagues around the globe.

Awards and accolades followed, and like an addict looking for a fix, he chased them with unbridled ambition. Steven worked harder and harder, often seven days a week. He poured himself into his career, while his wife focused on the home and raising their daughter. She supported his long hours and late nights at work. Life was just fine, or so it seemed.

Flash-forward three years. Steven was on a business trip to attend a convention where he was to receive another award for his accomplishments. After receiving the award, he and the group settled down to listen to a talk by the keynote speaker, who also happened to be a noted child psychologist. The speaker opened with a story about a study he had done long ago.

The story, as Steven shared it, had to do with a project to help kids be more focused in the classroom. What the researchers did was really quite simple. When kids raised their hands, sat in their chairs, and spoke when called on, they would earn a little token—a small object like a poker chip. And if they were disruptive, they'd lose a token. At the end of the day, all the kids in the classroom could cash out their tokens for small prizes. This continued for several weeks.

The token system worked like a charm. Disruptive classroom behaviors vanished. Kids were learning and paying attention. Seeing the success of this little intervention, the research team decided it was time to slowly fade out the prizes, and eventually there were no more prizes given for tokens earned during the day.

Now if you're guessing that this backfired, you'd be wrong. Even without the prizes, the kids continued to work extremely hard for the tokens, although they had no value and were essentially meaningless.

With that punch line, Steven sank into his chair and stared blankly at the plaque sitting in his lap. "Is this a meaningless token?" he wondered. And with a clarity he hadn't had before, he saw that he was just like those little kids, chasing things that didn't matter all that much in the end.

He knew that chase. He'd been chasing professional successes, recognition of his value and self-worth, approval, status and prestige, and on and on. He was a master at collecting tokens. Awards littered his office walls and bookshelves. Yet none of it ever satisfied a burning emptiness inside. In this watershed moment, Steven began to ask himself, "What really matters in my life?"

But old habits die hard, and sometimes we need a nudge. Sunday morning after his trip, Steven was once again getting ready to head into the office, as he usually did. As he was gathering his things, his three-year-old daughter approached and clung to his leg. He looked down at her, and she looked back up at him.

As he stooped down to say good-bye with a hug and peck on the cheek, his daughter whispered, "Does Daddy have to work today?" And with that, Steven felt his heart being ripped out of his chest. He knew the answer: No, he didn't have to work today.

There, in that moment and in those little eyes, Steven saw his legacy as a father and his lasting impact on this world. It was staring him right in the face. How would she remember him? How would others remember him? What would be his lasting impact on her life and on the world?

These questions made him see that he wanted to make a difference in the lives of others, and this was to become the guiding force steering Steven's life choices. In this way, he discovered his values, his role in the grand scheme of life, and his enduring legacy.

This epiphany was no accident. Like a perfect storm, things came together. Memories from long ago surged in like a tidal wave. He was propelled to his childhood, recalling how his dad was always at the office and how that hurt. And replaying in his head were his father's dying words: "Son, don't be like me... Life's too short. Make it count... Don't work as hard as I did. Nobody will give a hoot if you didn't spend an extra day at the office... Be there for your little angel...your wife...other people... Be there for them... That's the most important thing in this life. Those relationships will outlast you. People will remember you for what you did with them and for them... I wish I learned that long ago. I'm sorry I wasn't there for you when you were growing up."

This was the final straw, the kick in the pants that led Steven to say enough is enough. Steven never worked on weekends again. He made a choice to protect that time for his wife and daughter.

You may feel as though you're living a life like Steven's—chasing tokens that seem so important now but won't matter that much in the end. If so, this book may offer you a way to fill your life with authentic satisfaction, not more hollow tokens.

A Rudderless Ship

Ships require a compass to guide them and a rudder for steering. Life demands that too, and when we don't have an internal compass—an abiding sense of direction—to help us navigate, we can feel adrift, not knowing where to go or how to get there. This is where Karen found herself at age thirty.

As she put it, she had spent most of her life bouncing from one thing to the next. She bounced in and out of friendships, intimate relationships, apartments, schools, jobs and career interests, and hobbies.

Fearful and reluctant to make any significant life decisions, she settled into routines of circumstances and habits. This left her with a sense that life was happening to her, around her, and despite her. From the outside, it looked like Karen was living a rich life, but for her it was a life full of stress and busyness and lacking any clear purpose or vision, and it had more or less been that way for about fourteen years.

On her thirtieth birthday, she had a celebration with friends. After things quieted down that night, it dawned on Karen that nothing much had changed since she was an idealistic sixteen-year-old. She had her dreams and was desperate for something different but had no idea what that different would be.

Deep inside, Karen knew that she had always wanted to be about something, but she couldn't get past feeling too fearful, disorganized, apathetic, and full of excuses. She knew that goals were important, but was unable to set them for herself. She was reacting and surviving, rather than living and thriving. For a long time, she'd been telling herself that there's always tomorrow for dreams to come true.

Karen's thirtieth birthday led her to stop and look at what she'd become, and she didn't like what she saw. She realized that she'd put more time into planning her birthday party than she'd devoted to planning her life up until now. That little insight led her to take a bold step. She had to find her rudder and start steering her life, or risk continuing with a life of unfulfilled dreams, empty ambitions, and repeated yesterdays.

So Karen started seeking out opportunities where she might make a difference. She started with her community, volunteering at a local hospital to comfort children with terminal cancer. This experience left her feeling connected, empowered, and alive. It also rekindled her passion for working with children. That passion eventually led her halfway around the world and onto the streets of some of the poorest nations on this planet. For several years she worked tirelessly to administer polio vaccines to children living in extreme poverty. Now Karen is studying to be a doctor so she can make even more of a difference in the lives of young children.

Many people feel like Karen did—a bit rudderless. Uncertainty about your job and your life in general is very stressful. Knowing that many others are in the same boat is of little comfort. Karen eventually found her rudder by taking a bold step and creating a life consistent with her values.

Now is the perfect time for you to take a close look at your life and figure out what you really want to be doing. Are you drifting? Are you playing it safe by sailing your ship close to the shoreline? Maybe it's time to steer the boat out and challenge yourself to see where your strengths really lie. Or perhaps you feel that life has taken the wind out of your sails, leaving you defeated and deflated and lacking a clear vision or direction. This may be an opportunity to take stock and reclaim your life ship while you can.

Stuck in Quiet Desperation

We are all creatures of repetition and habit, and this can leave us feeling stuck. We have dreams and ambitions, but sometimes it seems as though we're caught on a carousel going round and round and never moving forward.

There are many ways to feel stuck. We can feel stuck in a job, or stuck in a marriage or a relationship, knowing that it isn't working and yet unable to see a way forward. We can feel stuck in a role or obligation, chained to what we have to do, are expected to do, and feel we must do. We can feel stuck in our aging bodies, stuck in the foods we tend to eat and those we avoid, or stuck in tired routines that leave us unfulfilled, wanting for more, and not knowing how to get it.

We can also feel stuck in our own heads, replaying countless old hurts or clinging to memories of sweet moments that have slipped away like ether. We can get stuck in painful thoughts and emotions, illness and disability, assets and aspirations. And we can get stuck in our limitations and unmet needs. The pain of life may be too much to bear, so we retreat into the comfort of old patterns to sip the elixir of relative safety and predictability once again.

Yet even this is small comfort. There is a powerful sense of unease linked with being stuck, something that Charlie knew all too well. At age twenty-five, he'd already settled into a life of routines, unmet expectations, and unfulfilled dreams. He'd seen his fair share of therapists and had been on and off a half dozen medications. But it hadn't always been this way.

As a teenager, Charlie was an exceptional musician and quite a mechanic. He played several instruments, wrote wonderful songs, and played in a band. When he wasn't doing that, he was pouring himself into his second love: old cars. He owned a 1969 Chevy

Chevelle and had single-handedly rebuilt its engine more than once in his parent's garage. He was that good.

If you'd asked Charlie then what he wanted to do with his life, he would have told you that he wanted to do something creative using his musical and mechanical talents. But his parents had different ideas. They wanted him to go to college, become a doctor, and then find someone to settle down with and start a family.

To avoid a major falling out with his parents, Charlie tried to live up to their expectations. He went to college but felt he was just going through the motions. And it turned out that going through the motions wasn't working either.

As a pre-med major, Charlie was skimming by with a C average and struggling with bouts of anxiety and depression. He was angry and resentful at times, and at other times he was completely stalled by apathy. His calls home became less frequent, and messages left by his parents usually went unanswered.

Alcohol and the occasional joint gave him a honeymoon from the pain and despair but never resolved the unease he was feeling. Eventually Charlie landed himself in a rehab program—far from college, and far from where he wanted to be with his life.

He was at a tipping point. He knew he was living a lie and suffocating in quiet desperation. He'd let go of *his* dreams, and for that he'd paid a steep price. He wasn't being true to his own passions and interests. He was imploding and suffering physically and emotionally. The joy had been sucked out of him, and he knew it.

He had to get back to his core. But first he would have to let go of blaming his parents and accept responsibility for how he lived his life. Only then would he have the freedom to use his creative talents with music and cars.

Charlie called a meeting with his parents, knowing full well that they wouldn't be crazy about what he had to say. Still, he did it. And like an avalanche, the weight of a decade of falsehood slid off his shoulders. This was the prize for being true to himself, and what made the risk worthwhile.

Charlie did finish college but changed his major to business. He remained sober throughout, and he eventually opened up his own auto shop. He joined a band, and on weekends they played at local clubs. Charlie's path was bittersweet—both painful and vital. In the end it left Charlie stronger and with a deepened sense of what mattered to him.

Feeling stuck or trapped can be a red flag, signaling that you're off course, perhaps doing things that don't really matter to you. Charlie's story shows the costs of living someone else's idea of what your life should be. If this sounds like you, now would be a good time to take stock. And even if your experience of being stuck is quite different from what Charlie went through, you can still use it as an opportunity to grow and move forward in more vital ways. We'll do our best to help you with that as you read on.

Suffering Amidst Hungry Lions

We are living in difficult times. Many people are suffering right now. You may be one of them. People are out of work, losing their homes, struggling to get by, and wondering how they'll make ends meet. And even if they still have a job and a home, they worry about their future and the well-being of their families, their children, and the planet. Many of these concerns are timeless and have been with us since the dawn of recorded history—and probably longer.

But struggles, challenges, and fears extend far beyond our own lives, our own local reach. We're also faced with daily reminders of the suffering of other human beings, the unpredictability and seeming inevitability of pain and our own capacity to suffer. You'll see this locally and more globally with poverty and homelessness, wars and violence, disease and illness, famine and starvation, and accidents and natural disasters.

We suffer in other, less tangible ways, too, through stigmatization, prejudice, marginalization, objectification, and dehumanization. You'll see it in your home, your workplace, the grocery store, the playground, and in areas of life that you care deeply about. You'll experience it yourself in times of anger, anxiety, depression, sadness, disappointment, regret, loss, death, illness, or despair. Just about everything we do can be touched by suffering.

All human beings carry the capacity to suffer in innumerable ways. We can suffer about a past that once was, our present circumstances, and a future that is yet to be. We can suffer about what we look like, what we think, what we remember, what we feel, and what we do. We can suffer in trying to be something or someone other than who we are, to feel something other than what we feel, or to think better, differently, or not at all. And we can suffer in good times just as easily as in bad. Suffering has been with us for as long as we know. Good fortune or economic recovery is no protection from this simple truth.

We can also struggle with our own pain and suffering, or the suffering of others, to the point where we end up like Charlie, feeling stuck, with no way out. Powerless to move forward, we remain on the sidelines. We watch as our suffering grows larger and becomes more central and our lives shrink around us to the size of a postage stamp. This can leave even the best of us feeling alone and disconnected from what matters.

It's so easy to lose sight of what matters in difficult times. In a way, it's like living in a world filled with big, hungry lions. Evolution has prepared us to protect ourselves in such a world, and as a result we are quite good at focusing all of our attention and energies on the lions in our midst. As we go into self-preservation mode, we narrow and harden. This keeps us safe—at least when we're actually in danger of being harmed or eaten.

But in the modern world most of us don't have to face real lions. We do have to face our own pain and suffering and that of others. In a sense, this is the psychological equivalent of having a hungry lion or two following us wherever we go. And as those hungry lions pull for our attention and energy, our attention shifts to the suffering and away from doing what matters. In that shift, the rest of the world—full of so many other things to look at and do—washes away. We lose our bearings, and our lives become about avoiding and managing our lions—our pain and suffering.

You'll notice that we didn't offer a personal story here. The story of the lions is a story about all of us. The three of us have our lions, and you do too. We all have the capacity to suffer. And despite the trappings of the modern world, filled with numerous technological advances and creature comforts, we haven't found a healthy way to escape human suffering. Nobody has that magic solution.

Notice that this isn't just about walking away. Heck, if the solution to suffering was like pulling your hand back from a hot stove, we'd say, "Do it. Just pull back and walk away." (And if we were speaking about real lions, we'd say do the same—and do it fast!) But this isn't the solution to human suffering. When we walk away from our suffering, we also tend to walk away from things that matter to us. So walking away has costs that can deeply diminish your life.

Maybe you feel as though your suffering has taken over your life. Or perhaps your experience is that pain and suffering have eclipsed any sense of what matters to you. The hurt has become central. You just don't know what you care about anymore.

Or maybe you're like millions of other people and do have a sense of what matters. Yet when you take a step forward, the lions pop up out of nowhere and threaten to eat you alive. So, tired and frustrated, you retreat into the comfortable and safe. Maybe you're looking for a way out of this cycle and back into your life.

If any of this resonates with you, you're not alone. And while we can't promise you a way to kill off your lions or lock them away, we can offer you a way to tame them so that you can move forward in ways that matter to you.

An Invitation

Our intention is to help you live a more empowered life. Whatever your motivation, you cannot escape the fact that each day affords you about 86,400 seconds to use as you wish—well, 57,600 if you want to get a good night's sleep. You can't bank time to use another day. The time you fail to use to good purpose, you lose. That's how it works.

Now, if life were a game where you were told that each day you'd be given $86,400 dollars to use as you wish or else lose, most people would find a way to spend every last dime. So how are you using your coin of time? And how would you like to use it? Are you using your time to create a life that matters to you?

Each day the clock resets and you are given another 1,440 minutes to use as you wish. That's about the amount of time it would take you to read this book. We certainly think that you're worth that amount of time. We invite you to take a look and see for yourself.

The Purpose of This Book

We wrote this book for the millions of people whose achievements, expectations, and goals have left them with a sense of emptiness or being unfulfilled—a feeling of ennui best described by Peggy Lee's immortal line "Is that all there is?" This feeling often grows stronger and darker with time and leaves people wondering what they did wrong. Where is their vitality, their engagement with life? What happened to the dreams and hopes they started out with?

The three of us have been there and have learned some valuable lessons about how to turn this situation around. We'll offer you both an explanation for this discontent and a solution. In our limited time on this planet, we've encountered thousands of people from all walks of life. And we've yet to meet anyone who hasn't experienced some life dissatisfaction leading to questions about what it all means and what truly matters.

From these encounters, we've noticed a recurring problem that cuts to the core of whether people are living a life that matters. The problem is this: Everyone wants to live a rich and meaningful life, but we get mired in setting goals and directions that are disconnected from our core values and the kind of life we truly want to lead. People are working hard, but often at things that don't really matter to them. Meanwhile, the things they truly care about are left unattended to or receive only a fraction of the time and energy they deserve. When our activities don't support our deepest values, we feel lost, adrift, and rudderless—sometimes even frantic.

To reclaim our engagement with life, we must find what matters. This book looks at three broad categories of life where we can benefit from being guided by our values: self-growth, service, and life purpose. Like the legs of a three-legged stool, each provides crucial support, and when one leg is broken, you'll tend to be out of balance or may even collapse. So we'll look at each area thoroughly and give you a chance to explore how all three apply to your life.

Knowing your values is an important start, but it's not enough. The emptiness and ennui won't go away unless you turn values into clear intentions, and intentions into committed actions. But this is hard to do. Most people can get from values to intentions easily enough, but stumble in jerks and fits when they try to turn their intentions into actions. This is where people tend to get stuck, spinning their wheels.

We get stuck because every step in a valued direction can be costly and painful. Doing what matters is hard for this reason. In fact, it often requires us to deal with thoughts and feelings we'd much rather avoid—the lions dwelling between our ears and in our hearts. We may have to face difficult emotions, like fear; painful thoughts, like "I'm going to fail"; and behavioral barriers, like not having the knowledge or resources to proceed. All flow from our history and are carefully orchestrated in our brain and central nervous system.

But here's the deal: Living your intentions by acting upon them—*and* accepting the costs—is how you create a life worth living. If you let the costs erode your values, you won't live your life on purpose. You'll end up like the characters in the Dr. Seuss book *Oh, the Places You'll Go*, just waiting. Waiting for life to begin.

We're going to show you how to tackle your roadblocks head-on so that you can move forward as you take action on your intentions in valued directions. There's a chapter on each of these barriers—cognitive, emotional, and behavioral—each with many techniques to help you overcome them. You'll see that the key to moving in valued directions hinges on a set of skills that can be packaged in one word: "willingness." As you grow in willingness, you'll learn to accept necessary pain and open up to it in the service of doing what you truly care about. This is how you tame your lions and get your life on track.

Working with this book, like anything worthwhile, involves a series of steps. Life is like that too: a series of steps on many paths that add up to something in the end—a life lived well, or not. We'll help you set a course toward engagement and vitality, but only you can do the work of putting what you read into practice.

This is a call to action—and a challenge. You determine how you'll live, not necessarily how you will die. Suicide, of course, is the exception, but that's a deliberate termination of a life on purpose, not living a life on purpose. And if you're lucky enough to live to a ripe old age, there will come a time when you'll look back on your life and reflect, as so many people do. Some will end up thinking, "Is that all there is?" Others will smile and think, "What a wonderful life!" These outcomes depend on what you do now. The choice is up to you. Now is the time to do something to make your life matter. We think you can do that.

Chapter 2

Why Values Matter

When you are inspired by some great purpose, some extraordinary project, all your thoughts break their bonds: Your mind transcends limitations, your consciousness expands in every direction, and you find yourself in a new, great, and wonderful world. Dormant forces, faculties and talents become alive, and you discover yourself to be a greater person by far than you ever dreamed yourself to be.

—Patanjali

You have brains in your head. You have feet in your shoes. You can steer yourself in any direction you choose.

—Dr. Seuss

You only live once—but if you work it right, once is enough.

—Joe E. Lewis

Imagine that you're driving somewhere in farm country, down long, straight lanes that eventually arrive at a crossroad. The road is unsigned, known only to the locals, or perhaps it has a name, but it means nothing without a map. At the junction, you are faced with a choice to go in one of three directions. But you aren't quite sure where you're going, and you have no map. You're lost, forced to make arbitrary choices based on the feel or look of the road, or based on some inviting object in the distance or the way the light strikes the pavement.

This is how we live life when our actions aren't guided by our values. Our choices become capricious and nearsighted, based simply on avoiding pain or seeking pleasure in the moment. We drift, uncertain of our direction and confused by every fork in the road.

When we know what matters, when we experience in our hearts and have words for what we care about, the crossroads feel different. Because we know where we're going, we have a clear and constant sense of direction that tells us when to turn and when to go straight.

Values Guide Us on Our Journey, and Goals Keep Us Moving

Knowing what matters is critical to creating a life of meaning and vitality. It's the way we steer; it's our compass. But a compass setting is a direction, not a goal. When we reach a goal, that particular journey is complete. With values, we set a course on a never-ending journey. You'll never be done with them as long as you're alive. It's something like heading west. You can keep going, and going, and going and never get there. Ridiculous sounding? Sure. But values are like that—there's always more to do.

Here are some examples to help bring this down to earth: Buying a house is a time-limited goal. Making a healthy, happy home for your family is a value, a direction. Learning to play guitar is a goal. Having a life in which you make music is a valued direction. Getting a teaching job is a goal. Doing meaningful work is a value that could run, like a golden thread, through your whole life. You travel in a valued direction by means of individual goals, but a value is more than the sum of the goals that support it. The value is what links them, gives them purpose, and makes them matter.

We Choose Our Core Values

There are universal values that hold the fabric of society together and keep us safe. Beyond that, though, what matters varies quite a bit from person to person. There's no single, overarching value that everyone's life should be about. The universe of possible valued directions is vast, and limited only by your imagination and your knowledge of what's important to you. So how do you recognize *your* core values and find the unique paths that *your* life needs to take?

Philosopher Thomas Aquinas talked about the difference between what he called first freedom and second freedom. First freedom is a state of potential, with a vast array of choices laid out before us. Second freedom is where we forsake these limitless possibilities and focus on a very few. First freedom is full of excitement and unlimited possibility, but it's a state where very little happens. You need the particular choices of second freedom for life to take shape and begin to *be* anything.

The same dichotomy exists in the world of values. So many things could matter to us. Some people care about saving the planet, and others care about orphaned dogs. Some people's lives seem focused on the welfare of immediate family, and others yearn for sweeping reforms and social justice. Some people seek to learn, embracing every new experience. Others want to teach, imparting skills and wisdom. Some love beauty and yearn to create it. Others want to just make things work efficiently and see that as a kind of beauty.

All the possible things that *could* matter to you are essentially first freedom. The world beckons with problems and fascinations and countless things that could be done. Your gut feelings can provide helpful guidance in choosing the things you'll value most from among all of the possible directions. Just as you recognize the special people and things you love as being different from others, a feeling of "rightness" helps you know what you most value. In the same way, your basic intuition can speak to you about life directions that are uniquely fitting for you. When you feel good about some choices and sad about others, those gut feelings of "alignment" or "misalignment" can help you identify life directions that are uniquely your own.

The "rightness" we're speaking of here isn't a *moral* rightness. It's your intuition, an inner voice, a basic wisdom everyone can tap into that helps penetrate the uncertainties of life. This feeling often shows up as a sense of being in alignment with your higher self. Sometimes it comes as a sense of peace or ease, a simple knowing. If all of this seems unfamiliar or unclear, don't worry. The next three chapters are devoted to helping you identify your core values.

The bottom line is this: If you listen to what you feel at each choice point and crossroads, the sum of all of what you learn is your values: core, strong, unyieldingly yours.

Finding vs. Living Your Values

Knowing what matters is a critical first step, but there's an even more important second step: *doing* what matters. All of us have experienced regret about times when we were clear about a valued course we should have taken but didn't. As a rule, we upbraid ourselves about our laziness or cowardice in these situations. But this may be unfair.

Doing what matters in the pursuit of a values-based life can be costly. We may pay in the coin of fear and potential failure. We sometimes pay by facing disapproval and rejection, or by having to forsake other needs that are painful to ignore. And living a values-based life often demands that we face the demons of our own self-judgment and shame.

All of this can seem like wading through a mucky, ominous swamp. On the other side you see what you wish for, but to get there you need to take a bold step into the muck, the stench, and the uncertainty of the swamp. It's uncomfortable and messy, but you're in the muck for a reason. You aren't wading through the swamp just for the sake of doing so. Something precious to you lies on the other side, something that calls out to you and that you want in life.

The only way to get that precious thing, whatever it may be, is by forging through the swamp. Life is often this way. As we step in the direction of what we want, we risk getting something we'd rather not have. Yet if we hand over our lives in return for relative calm and safety, we can end up just standing on the shore, waiting, wanting, and longing for a life that seems beyond reach.

Barriers Between You and Your Values and Purpose

From time to time, everyone will face nasty swamps and seemingly insurmountable barriers in life. These barriers can leave us disheartened, with a sense that life is nothing more than an endless litany of one painful experience or disappointment after another. But life doesn't have to be that way.

If you're interested in doing what matters, you'll need to understand what gets in your way, then face those blocks and move forward with them, rather than coming to a standstill and getting stuck. For now, let's focus on what the obstacles are, and later on we'll show you how to deal with them. While obstacles can take many ominous forms, they arise from just three sources: thoughts, emotions, and behaviors.

The First Obstacle Is Your Mind

Everyone's mind produces a constant waterfall of thoughts. These thoughts help us survive by predicting the future, solving problems, and making judgments. But while all of these cognitive functions are useful, they can also become hobgoblins that frighten or paralyze us. When we start to choose valued directions, our minds can predict catastrophe or pass judgment on our choices (or just about anything, for that matter).

Jeff could tell you exactly what it's like having a mind that turns on you. He went through a bitter divorce and hasn't seen much of his ten-year-old daughter since moving out ten months ago. He wants to be an involved father; he wants to watch his child grow up. But his mind says something else: "She's mad at you. She's going to act pissy if you call. She probably won't come to the phone. You screwed this up so bad, there's no fixing it. It will feel awkward. Your ex will offer one of her patented insults."

This is a perfect example of how the mind tries to predict disaster or judge our behavior. Its purpose is to keep us from taking risks and out of potential trouble. Its message is clear: "No matter how important a choice is from the point of view of your values, don't do it." That would be great advice if you were about to put yourself in a situation that would leave you maimed or dead, but not here—not with Jeff, and not with his values.

The Second Obstacle Stems from Emotions

Feelings of fear, shame, emptiness, loss, or aloneness are common when choosing to do what matters. When painful emotions get linked with what we care about, we can end up stuck or headed in another direction. Being paralyzed with fear is exactly what kept Janet stuck.

Soon after she started working at a printing company, she wanted to push the company to be more green. Using soy inks and recycled paper were just two of the ideas she had in mind. But the thought of speaking up at a meeting triggered a fear of ridicule. So she decided to write a letter to her boss. But as she began writing, it felt somehow dangerous, like she was making herself a target or putting her job at risk. She tried writing the letter a dozen times, but her sense of foreboding eventually won out. Now months have gone by and her company still hasn't made any changes.

Sam, a patent lawyer, was caught in a similar emotional bind. He yearned to do something that would allow him to express himself creatively. He took a fiction writing class, but setting evenings aside to work on his stories proved difficult. Whenever he tried to write and was deprived of friends and camaraderie, he felt oddly empty. He also struggled with a fear of failure: What if he read his story to the class and became a target of criticism? While creativity was an important value, Sam began to realize it could have a cost. If he was going to write anything, the experience would include feelings of loneliness and vulnerability. Before too long, he dropped out of the class.

The Third Obstacle Is Behavioral

Behavior is anything you can do. Sometimes what we do stands in our own way, and other times we just don't know what to do. The latter may be nothing more than a skills deficit—you simply don't know how to do the thing that matter to you.

That's where Alisha, whose mother had Alzheimer's, found herself. She wanted to remain close, to somehow give her mother the feeling that she was safe and cared for. But her mom no longer recognized her and seemed lost in her own world. Staying close required learning a new skill. Alisha had to learn how to contact her mom on the physical level, entering her world through small, visceral experiences and pleasures.

Sometimes behavioral obstacles are a matter of logistics. Scheduling problems, costs, distances, or the needs of others may get in the way. Frank, a master carpenter, knew all about logistical blocks. He had created a design for a uniquely beautiful bed. This wasn't just a mattress platform, but an environment that fostered intimacy, peace, and spiritual awakening. It was one amazing place to sleep. The problem was, he had to work on the beds after a long, fifty-hour workweek, during times when his family clamored for attention. On top of that, the beds cost money to build and took time to sell. It felt like nothing but struggle to make and share his beautiful creation.

Why Doing What Matters Doesn't Get Done

Given the power of cognitive, emotional, and behavioral blocks, it isn't surprising that we often abandon our values and cast our lives adrift. Sometimes it's just too hard to keep going, to keep trying—to keep feeling the pain that a values-based life requires us to face.

Instead, we run toward the shelter of brief pleasures and numbing routines, toward the safe harbor of each ordinary day. However much these moments may ease or soothe us, we're left without meaning, miles from doing the things that matter most.

There is a way out of this cycle, but first we need to face the problem squarely. The central problem is this: All of us have a tendency to pour our attention, energy, and resources into feeling better. This is understandable, because we've all been taught from an early age on that if we feel bad, we should do something to feel better.

Sometimes this works, and, in fact, it works just often enough to draw us in again and again, like when you take an aspirin for a headache or drown your sorrows in a drink. Those solutions may work in the short term, but they don't address any underlying problems. And everything we know about emotions tells us that they aren't something we can just flip on and off like a light switch. If that were possible, most of us would gorge on happiness 24/7, and a great deal of suffering would cease to exist.

The illusion that we can and ought to control our emotions is so entrenched in our culture that we tend to take it for granted and lose sight of other alternatives. In fact, polls show that when you ask people what's important to them, they'll often say things like "I want to feel happier," "I want to feel more confident," "I want people to respect me," or "I want to be calmer and more at peace."

All of these statements sound like values, but they're really emotional goals masquerading as values. And as goals, they're a setup. They can never be achieved or held in any enduring way. And they aren't things, though we often treat them as such. We'd like to have and hold more of the good feelings and keep the bad ones out. It's natural, but it's also a trap and a one-way street into disappointment and despair.

You set yourself up for disappointment if you make feeling better—happier, more confident, more accepted, whatever—the reason for your actions. Chances are, sometimes you'll feel better about yourself once you start moving in the direction of your values. But sometimes you won't. And sometimes it can hurt to do what matters.

When you do things just to feel better, you're walking on thin ice, because no matter what you do, you won't always feel good, calm, confident, or accepted. So much of life, and especially the behavior of other people, is uncertain. And feelings are fickle. They come and go, morphing and changing like the weather. And they can be just as unpredictable as the weather, too. That's why they're a weak foundation for your choices and actions.

It's no wonder that we get lost, that things we care about are replaced by things that merely comfort us. Values-based choices require a commitment to feel and experience whatever that choice brings. We must face our monsters, however big and however scary. Willingness is the key to silencing the monsters so that they don't lead us astray.

Willingness

Willingness means accepting everything that happens when we set off in a valued direction. It's a commitment to keep going despite problems and emotions we'd rather avoid. Willingness says, "I will feel whatever I feel, whatever pleasure or pain, whatever doubt or failure or satisfaction. I will not run away or give up; I will stay this course, no matter what I think or feel."

Notice that the root of the word "willingness" is "will." Will is intention becoming action. Will turns wanting into doing. Willingness is all of that, plus the conscious awareness of costs. Doing something requires effort, risk, and pushing past our natural resistance. So willingness is facing the cost of a valued action—and doing it anyway.

Why persist despite the costs? The intention or desire to do something is a far cry from doing it. And an absence of willingness is often why we fail to act on our values. Willingness acknowledges that every step down a path that matters takes effort—and requires us to face formidable obstacles.

Consider the costs that Eleanor faced. Her son was struggling academically, and a teacher advised that he needed help at home. That seemed reasonable. But the first time Eleanor tried to oversee an algebra assignment, it was a nightmare. Eleanor initially thought, "I can't do this. I don't know enough to help." Then came the boredom of struggling through problem after problem, and tiredness from a long day capped by a longer night. Plus, her son was ungrateful and often resisted her suggestions.

Here are all of the blocks we outlined above: cognitive ("I can't do this"), emotional (boredom, tiredness, and resentment), and behavioral (not knowing much about math or how to deal with resistant children). Without willingness, blocks like these can quickly overwhelm our motivation. Often we give up. But not always.

Eleanor kept helping her son with his homework. She turned on her willingness because of her values around parenting. And she did that with her boredom, tiredness, and discouraging thoughts, and with a gloomy child along for the journey. Eleanor's willingness grew out her conviction that her son's future was important, and this made it possible to live with a certain amount of pain along the way.

Willingness shapes all of our lives, and in doing so it shapes history. Charles Darwin was hideously seasick throughout his five-year travels on the HMS *Beagle*. He pressed on—with his seasickness—because he had a purpose clearly in mind. He was working in a field he loved and gathering evidence about geologic and biologic processes—evidence that would eventually inform his groundbreaking book *On the Origin of Species*. He was willing to suffer on a sea-tossed ship because science mattered. For all of us, pain is often a part of living the life we care about.

Willingness is something you do, and you can't do it partially or halfway. You're either willing—100 percent willing—to live your values, or you aren't. If you're only a little willing to feel pain, soon enough you'll reach a point where you give up. Darwin was 100 percent willing to be seasick—day in, day out—in his quest for scientific knowledge. He didn't make a deal with the captain to drop him in Tahiti if the nausea got too bad.

Sam, our patent lawyer and aspiring fiction writer, quit writing because he wasn't willing to bear the emotional cost: feelings of loneliness and vulnerability and fear of failure. To write alone at night, to read his stories to the class, demanded 100 percent willingness to feel what had to be felt while writing night after night and while sharing what he had written with others.

Willingness doesn't mean you won't struggle with thoughts and feelings that run counter to your values or obstruct your path. It just means that, on a deeper level, you know you're committed to staying on course, and you do it for a reason: The underlying value really matters to you, and it matters more than the blocks.

How We Stand with Our Pain Matters

We've looked at how cognitive, emotional, and behavioral blocks can make living your values painful. But what happens if you steer away from valued directions to avoid that pain? The result is usually a different kind of pain. Instead of fear, you may feel guilt, shame, discontent, or despair. Instead of effort and struggle, you experience a loss of meaning. That hurts, as does not living your life the way you wish.

So there's no getting away from it. Avoiding a valued path creates a deeper pain, a pain of the worst kind, a pain that threatens the core of your identity. It creates the feeling that something is wrong with your life, your choices, your relationships, and your very self. Over time, this can lead to dark regrets and a sense of having failed in the things that are most important. The only way out of this pain is to identify your core values and then act on them.

This book will help you do two important things so you can act on your values: The first is to see the obstacles clearly—to know exactly what you'll have to feel and think and struggle with. The second is to find a way to answer yes to this question: Are you willing to have whatever pain it may take to be what you want to be in your life? This commitment can only be real, can only be valid, when you fully understand and accept the natural and inevitable pain of life. Nothing less will give you a life that matters.

Chapter 3

Pursuing Self-Growth Values

I can't change the direction of the wind, but I can adjust my sails to always reach my destination.

—Jimmy Dean

I find the great thing in this world is not so much where we stand, as in what direction we are moving.

—Oliver Wendell Holmes

Only I can change my life. No one can do it for me.

—Carol Burnett

What do you want your life to stand for? What really matters to you? These perennial questions are important, because to live your life, you need to know what you're living it for. That's why we start with self-growth values.

We understand that it may seem odd to start with self-growth, perhaps even selfish, but there are good reasons for beginning here. You might think of it like that familiar caution to put on your own oxygen mask before assisting others. Also, you need to understand who you are and who you want to be before you can most effectively reach out in service to others. Yet it's so easy to lose sight of self-growth values. And you may not even know what yours are.

Self-growth values can fall by the wayside when we're consumed with business, getting things done, meeting the needs of others, or bingeing. They can slip off our radar when we feel anxious, down, or simply unhappy with the way our lives are going. Instead of self-growth, we fixate on the pain and what we lack, and on attempts to feel better. And there are many ways to try to feel better, some destructive.

Yet nothing seems to do the trick. The pain never goes away for good. And when it seems to, a new pain often surfaces to take its place. This cycle of trying to feel better when we hurt can replay itself thousands of times in a lifetime, leaving us with a sense that we're spinning our wheels, forever looking for new solutions and never finding one that lasts. We end up stymied, feeling bad about ourselves, and dissatisfied with our lives.

So, what's the alternative? Maybe the alternative is as simple as knowing what you care about and letting that be your guide, or your North Star, as Martha Beck describes it in *Finding Your Own North Star: Claiming the Life You Were Meant to Live*.

If you look deeply inside yourself, you may be able to connect with several aspects of your life that are precious. You don't need to justify them and come up with reasons why they're so important to you. You just know it. You carry these values with you wherever you go, and they also remain with you despite changes in your emotional climate. Sure, it can seem like what you value gets obscured or hidden by circumstances, feelings, or thoughts, much like clouds may cover the stars on an overcast night. Still, you know the stars are there even when you can't see them. You also know with great certainty that the stars will be back in view eventually. Clouds don't stick around forever, but the stars surely will.

Your values are like the stars in a way. They remain fairly constant over time, and they are always present in the background. But there are countless stars in the sky, so you must identify which you'll look to, and which you'll use for guidance. In this chapter, we'll help you find your own stars.

Two Types of Values

In turns out that most human beings share some basic values. In fact, in one of the world's largest opinion polls on this topic, Gallup International asked fifty thousand people from sixty countries around the globe this basic question: "What matters most in life?"

And regardless of whether people lived in developing countries or nations with more conveniences and luxuries, the top two answers were the same: good health and a happy family life. Of course, there are individual variations, and you may not rank both values highly, but an interesting point here is that these represent the two main types of values: self-growth values and service values.

When we've asked people about what matters most, we've heard a wide range of responses. Some people say, "I want to be an engaged parent" or "I want to be a loving partner." Others say things like "I want to help people who are in difficult life situations" or "I'd like to have friends who can trust me and whom I feel close to." All of these statements are expressions of values that focus on relationships with other people. They are usually service oriented. We'll talk more about this type of value in the next chapter.

The other type of value is more personal, starting with you and your growth as a human being. Again, there are many possibilities. Some people focus on learning as an important self-growth value and wish to keep learning new things throughout life. As the Gallup poll showed, many consider their own health paramount and focus on being healthy and taking care of their body. Yet others express an abiding sense of wanting to be more in tune with nature, the environment, and the outdoors.

We've heard people express a passion for growing spiritually, whether through prayer and love of God or manifest in greater awareness and appreciation of themselves and the world. Some love the arts and wish for things like a life filled with music, while others enjoy personal challenges. All of these statements are expressions of self-growth values. Your self-growth values will involve you and your relationship with yourself—your mind, your body, your soul. They serve to enhance you, your creativity, and your quality of life.

Sometimes self-growth and service values are intertwined. For instance, when a young woman says, "I want to have a career where I can continue to develop myself and where I can make a real difference in the lives of others," she expresses two values: developing herself and supporting others. Likewise, when a man says, "I want to express myself through playing music," he's focused on enhancing the creative part of himself, but he may also care about sharing his music and creativity with others by playing for them.

Is It Okay to Pursue Self-Growth Values?

Many people wonder whether it might be self-indulgent to pursue self-growth values. This is an important question to ponder. When people start thinking and talking about directions for personal growth, they often feel a bit uneasy, and rushing in right behind the unease is a sense of guilt, even shame.

Our minds love making connections, and the fuel for the guilt is the linking of self-growth with selfishness and egocentrism. Framed in this way, your personal growth is outflanked by two undesirable traits—not good. It's hardly surprising that we feel guilt when those links are created.

But it doesn't stop there. Our minds then fan the flames with judgments: "You're not good enough!" "You don't deserve to do good things for yourself!" "You're being selfish!" "Why don't you focus on others instead of focusing on yourself?" If we allow those thoughts to take hold, we end up feeling awful about doing something we care about. This can keep us stuck in a rut, or, at best, we may move forward with great reluctance.

This is a key problem with self-growth values. The mind is putting up all kinds of roadblocks. When we listen to this chatter, naturally we get discouraged, and we may abandon important personal journeys before they even begin.

For now, what's important is to notice your mind doing what minds are designed to do. Don't let discouraging self-talk keep you from looking at your self-growth values. This mind chatter is just one layer of your experience. Think of your experience as being like an onion: As you peel back layer after layer, you'll eventually get to the core—even if there are some tears along the way—and connect with the pristine in you: your basic, innate goodness.

Think of this process as being like clearing out the clutter in your closet. You know there's something important buried underneath jumbled piles of stuff, even if you can't put your finger on what it is. As you go into this process more deeply, you'll discover things about yourself that you had forgotten or neglected, and maybe even some things you didn't know you had within you.

Don't turn away because the clutter seems too much or too hard to tackle. This isn't about the clutter. It isn't about dwelling on what's wrong with you or what needs to be fixed. It's about connecting with your values, and values are always whole, never broken. Your mind may judge them, but if you start to notice its chatter, you'll discover that it can judge just about anything. So, don't buy the chatter. You'll be left feeling broken or bereft if you let it take you to a place where you end up not living your values.

As you embark on this exploration, we aren't sure what you'll find, but we can say this: When people start moving in valued directions, they often feel better about themselves and their lives, in ways that are deep, not superficial.

So let's go back to the question we posed at the beginning of this section and answer it with a resounding yes! It's not only okay to consider your self-growth values, it's vitally important that you do so.

Whether you care about making something of your life, making a difference in the lives of others, or having something to share, you'll need to take care of your own house first. This doesn't mean you forgo your social or service values. This journey isn't about one being more important than the other.

You can have both self-growth and service values; there's no inherent conflict between them. And they do have something important in common: They all flow from you, from your center. When you take care of yourself, you're in a better position to reach out to others, share with them, and support them. And what better way to take care of yourself than to find out what matters to you and begin the process of living a life that matters. As you start to do this, others will see this about you. It may just embolden them to do the same. It's one of the kindest things you can do for yourself and others. So let's start there.

Connecting with Your Self-Growth Values

There are a number of domains or areas of life that revolve around developing and fostering the relationship you have with yourself. Each is important in its own right, but not all of them are important for everyone and not all of them will be important for you.

Of course, there are endless ways to categorize these domains, and life being what it is, the domains often overlap. The categories we present in this book are just one way of looking at it, but we've found that these categories work well. As you read the descriptions of each domain below, ask yourself, "Is this area important to me?" Identifying areas of life that are significant to you will give you a starting point for zeroing in on your unique self-growth values.

To help you with this process, we suggest you carefully consider each area and then ask yourself whether it's important to you or not. This is a yes or no kind of thing. Just look into your gut as you reflect. A "yes" means that an area is something you care about in your life, and a "no" means that the area doesn't matter all that much to you. Don't get too caught up with how you respond to each area; your answers aren't set in stone. You can always make adjustments later on. This process is just one way of helping you tease out where your important values lie, where to begin your values work, and what to devote time and effort to.

If you say yes to an area, meaning that it's important to you, then go on and rate how satisfied you are with your life in this area right now. A rating of 0 means you're not at all satisfied with your life in this area, 1 means you're moderately satisfied, and 2 means you're very satisfied.

We also encourage you to delve deeper into the areas you rate as important. To help you with this exploration, we've included questions in the descriptions below. Take some time with them. For each domain, we also include two brief examples from people we've known who were willing to share their self-growth intentions and a little bit about how those intentions played out in their lives.

Later on, we'll help you develop some valued intentions for yourself. An intention is simply a statement of how you'd like to live your life in a domain that you value and consider important. It should capture what's most essential and vital to you in that aspect of life.

Physical Self-Care and Health

How important is your physical health to you? What role do exercise and healthy eating play in your life? Why do you want to take care of your body, and what does it mean to you to do so through exercise and diet?

People have a variety of motivations for trying to stay healthy. Some do it out of sheer enjoyment; others do it in order to be successful in a physically demanding job. Still others see a healthy lifestyle as a way of taking care of themselves, perhaps so that they stand a better chance of living to a ripe old age and being around for those they love.

Think about what motivates you to stay healthy. There are many possible reasons for actively pursuing good health, and all are valid. What is it about caring for your physical well-being that appeals to you, and how important is it to you to act in accordance with this value?

Here's what Lyn, a single thirty-something from a very large family, came up with for her intention: "I spent so much time taking care of other people that I neglected to take care of myself. I now make sure my own needs are met. When I take care of myself, I'm better able to take care of others."

Craig, a thirty-nine-year-old personal athletic trainer, described what health means to him this way: "When my doctor told me I had high blood pressure about five years ago, I knew it was because of my hectic work schedule. I didn't want my work to screw up my health and create problems. So I decided to make some changes by slowing things down with my work routine. I also set my mind on getting myself in shape like I do when helping my clients, and I made aerobic exercise a part of my daily routine. Not only is this helping me feel better, my doctor told me that my blood pressure was coming down and without me having to take medication. Because of this experience, I now teach my clients about how stress can affect their health."

Yes   No   Is this area important to you? (Circle one.)

0   1   2   If it's important, how satisfied are you with your
                life in this area right now? (Circle one.)

Spirituality

We are all spiritual beings in a sense. This is true whether you practice a faith, pray, meditate, reflect and consider, ponder life's questions, or seek out ways to grow in awareness of yourself and your connections with other human beings and the world around you. So participating in an organized religion counts here, but for many people spirituality transcends the boundaries of a religion or church, or belief in a higher power.

Take a moment to reflect on your spirituality. Do it broadly and on your own terms, and don't limit yourself to cultural or social expectations. What seems most appropriate and suitable for you? Are there things larger than your own life that inspire you? What are the mysteries of life before which you stand in awe? Describe the role you'd like to see spirituality play in your life and how that would manifest. If you had this in your life, what kind of qualities would it provide for you?

Amelia, a middle-aged nutritionist, thought long and hard about this area and came up with this: "It's important for me to have a relationship with God and to make that a part of my daily life—to experience that I'm connected with a force that's larger than myself. It also gives me a sense of purpose and meaning, and leaves me with the feeling of not being so alone. Prayer helps me find an inner peace."

Melissa, a thirty-four-year-old office clerk shared this with us: "When I get angry, it's so easy for me to lose touch with my spiritual side. The guilt, shame, and hurt caused by my anger have left me feeling like my life has no meaning or purpose. I finally said enough is enough and decided to get back on track with my spiritual side. Prayer and meditation practice help me be more patient and have a sense of harmony and inner peace. Sometimes prayer gives me a sense of connection to a higher power; other times it's more local and focused on growth, peace, and connection with others."

Yes   No   Is this area important to you? (Circle one.)

0   1   2   If it's important, how satisfied are you with your life in this area right now? (Circle one.)

Creativity

What is it about your life that makes you feel like an artist? Like spirituality, creativity covers a lot of territory. We aren't talking exclusively about traditional artistic mediums like painting and making music, although these are popular ways people exercise their creativity. You can also think about how you like to cook, put together an outfit, do woodwork, knit, or write in a journal—then expand out from there. Life offers endless avenues to express your creativity. What place do creative activities have in your life, and how important are they to you?

Bob, a building contractor, spends many hours creating by building new homes and renovating older structures. As it turns out, construction is just one area where he has creative interests. He described it this way: "I want to express myself through painting. I get such a kick out of seeing where the brush wants to take me. I never ever sit down to paint with a creative intention. That would ruin it for me. The best part of painting is feeling like I'm a translator for the materials, that I'm telling their story and drawing attention to what people often don't see."

Geraldine, age sixty-one, worked many years as a loan officer at a bank. When she wasn't doing that, she was nurturing her expressive side at home. Here's what she told us: "I started working on the landscape behind my house several years ago, re-laying the stonework in the patio and planting new cypress trees along the edge of the property. I enjoy the creativity of gardening because I feel like I'm making whole new worlds. I just love making something new. This isn't about recreating a landscape you could find just about anywhere. I enjoy watching my efforts grow into something unique."

Yes   No   Is this area important to you? (Circle one.)

0   1   2   If it's important, how satisfied are you with your life in this area right now? (Circle one.)

Leisure and Play

The way you spend your leisure time can profoundly affect your quality of life, so it's important to consider it carefully. This domain can include just about anything. You can have a spirit of play outside of work, and at work too.

When children are playing for fun, they're doing much more than just having fun. Children love playing because it allows them to fully absorb themselves in activities that often call on all of their senses. Children also use play to express themselves—their feelings, moods, and dreams. But play isn't just for children! Adults can and often want to play for the same reasons that children do: to be fully absorbed in an activity that's fun and that allows them to express the playful and creative part of themselves.

In this domain, look for the value you place on expressing that playful spirit. Do you cherish having time to unwind, have fun, be a kid again, challenge yourself, or develop new interests? Any activity that has a playful quality counts here. So how would you describe the quality of this part of your life if it were exactly the way you would like it to be? And with that in mind, what activities, interests, or hobbies would you love to cultivate and explore if you could?

When thinking about this area, Henry, a fifty-six-year-old high school teacher, immediately knew the answer. Here's what he shared: "I want to lead a life that's filled with music. When I play or listen to my favorite music, it seems like my worries and 'issues' become much less important. That shows me what really matters in my life. I can get totally lost in my guitar playing and lose track of time. It's important for me to take time every day to play, not just for the music, but to relax and stay positive."

Melanie, a thirty-three-year-old stay-at-home mom, perked up when thinking about what she valued in this area. Here's what she said: "I want play to be a part of my life. Somewhere deep inside, I long to pick dandelions, dance in the rain, walk through a drive-through, and sing to the stars. Each day, I take time to celebrate life. Sometimes all this means is getting dirty in the sandbox with my five-year-old, but I'm also not above hiding the remote from my husband, or 'testing' the spaghetti by throwing it at the wall just one more time, even when I know it's ready to eat."

Yes   No   Is this area important to you? (Circle one.)

0   1   2   If it's important, how satisfied are you with your life in this area right now? (Circle one.)

Work and Career

Work may involve a paid job, unpaid volunteer work, or home-making. What's important to you about your work, and what qualities does having a job provide for you? For some people the answer is financial security, independence, or prestige; for others it involves intellectual challenge or interacting with or helping others.

Have you put a valued career or volunteer job on hold because of emotional or cognitive roadblocks? Maybe it's a fear of failure or sense of unease as you consider a career that may mean giving up some of the comforts or luxuries of your current lifestyle. Or maybe you think it would be irresponsible to pursue your dream job.

Don't let those thoughts and emotions stop you from exploring this area. After all, most of us spend a major chunk of our waking hours involved in work. There are many ways to make whatever you do personally rewarding. Keep that in mind as you envision your dream job or how you'd like to use your energy, talents, and skills productively. What would that look like? What would you do if you could be doing anything? Describe the qualities of a job or endeavor that you believe would be perfect for you.

Sharon, a middle-aged medical doctor, told us this: "I love intellectual challenges and being respected by others. Being a doctor gives me both. Sometimes it's like solving a puzzle when patients describe their symptoms but no diagnosis seems to fit. It's also important for me to feel like I'm making a difference. So every time a patient comes to me with unanswered questions or a colleague needs my advice on a diagnosis, I get a tangible sense of contribution and worth. I love sharing my opinions and being able to find helpful answers."

Carl, a thirty-something financial analyst, came up with this: "I couldn't stand working in the corporate world until I began to notice and ask questions about how much paper the office wasted every day. We didn't have any recycling bins, and people were getting handouts at meetings when overhead projectors could do the job. Eventually

I got so into researching corporate conservation plans that my boss put me in charge of recycling for the department, and eventually for the whole company. I didn't get a pay raise or a new title, but now I get excited when I go to the office because I'm doing something that's really important to me—helping the environment."

Yes   No   Is this area important to you? (Circle one.)

0   1   2   If it's important, how satisfied are you with your life in this area right now? (Circle one.)

Personal Growth and Education

Your personal growth is nurtured when you explore yourself and develop as a human being—emotionally, intellectually, physically, spiritually, behaviorally. This often means gaining a deeper sense of who you are. In fact, many of the domains you've already read about have everything to do with your personal growth as a human being.

Personal growth is often related to learning. Traditional schooling certainly counts, but growth and learning can happen just about anywhere. You don't need a classroom for that. For example, amateur athletes may experience health or social benefits from participating in a sport, but these activities can also offer a sense of being challenged and the pleasure of learning or refining a skill. So look within yourself and see if you can find anything about personal growth and learning that's important to you. Would you like to sharpen skills you already have, or develop new ones? Are there areas of competence you'd like to explore? Do you enjoy learning new things? Do you enjoy sharing what you've learned with others?

Jonathan, a thirty-nine-year-old police officer by trade, shared that he had a love for learning: "I had to learn Spanish for my job, but once I started taking the classes I found that I really enjoyed being in school again. I like how studying gives me a chance to expand my perspective on the world. I ended up going way beyond the classes required for my position, and I'm thinking that I may even pursue an advanced degree."

Brittany, a thirty-two-year-old nurse, told us this: "It's important to me to keep learning. From time to time, my friend and I enroll in local community classes or decide to try out a new hobby together. Right now, we're learning Chinese cooking. I feel lazy and stuck in one place if I'm not learning something new. To me, feeling like a whole person involves confronting new challenges and learning new things."

Yes   No   Is this area important to you? (Circle one.)

0   1   2   If it's important, how satisfied are you with your life in this area right now? (Circle one.)

Self-Kindness and Compassion

Many of us have old wounds from losses or unfair treatment by others, and, sadly, some have suffered abuse and trauma. These experiences can change us for good or for ill. So often the darkness is all we can see, and this makes us harden up. We blame ourselves or others and retreat from the world and all it has to offer. This ultimately hurts us.

The antidote is to practice acts of kindness and loving care—starting with yourself and then expanding out to other people in your life. This can help you stop being at war with yourself; it will also take the sting out of the psychological pain and unhappiness you've lived through and may continue to experience now. Even if you don't have much pain in your life, you still might value kindness and compassion.

How important is it to you to learn to be kinder to yourself? How would your life be different if you were to practice more acceptance and compassion toward your feelings, memories, and wounds? Do you look for ways to practice acts of kindness toward yourself, and if so, how does that look? What do you do? If you don't do this currently, what form might it take? Even if self-compassion seems difficult, does it seem important that you start moving in that direction?

Rachel, a forty-one-year-old social worker, gave this area a lot of thought. And then she offered this: "I spend a lot of time hearing about the pains and suffering of other people. And when I see that, it makes me want to shut down. I'm starting to see that I share the pains of my clients, even friends and family. And I really need to practice what I preach. Basically, be kinder and gentler with myself—even with my old regrets, fears, and worries—so that I can be helpful and connected with other people in my life in their moments of suffering and pain."

Paul, a fifty-two-year-old sales manager, shared this: "I want to be kinder to myself. Ever since high school I've blamed myself for not being 'good enough.' I did it in college, at my job, and even at home as a husband and father. It didn't matter how successful I was, it was never good enough. I was my own worst enemy. Through meditation and simple reflection, I could see this going on. So I started doing kind things for myself—and just because they're important to me. Now I think about what I can do to be good to myself each day. I feel a hell of a lot better because of it. My relationships at work and home are growing again too."

Yes   No   Is this area important to you? (Circle one.)

0 1 2   If it's important, how satisfied are you with your life in this area right now? (Circle one.)

Developing Your Self-Growth Intentions

It's time to pause and reflect a bit. Thinking about various domains of life and what matters to you within them is important, but it's just the first step in this journey. The next step is to move from thoughts to intentions.

Recall that an intention is simply a statement of how you'd like to live your life in an area that's important to you. It should capture the essence of what really matters to you in that area. And intentions should be real. They ought to genuinely reflect your personal wishes. This isn't about what others want you to do or expect you to do, what people have told you "should" or "must" do, or even what you've told yourself you "should" or "must" do.

Don't confuse intentions with goals. Intentions should reflect the directions in which you want to move—now and for the foreseeable future. Unlike goals, they have no end point. With intentions, you'll never be able to say, "Now I've accomplished that," or check them off like you might with items on a grocery list or a to-do list. Instead, see your intentions as a never-ending story. Let them speak to how you want to live every day of your life in areas that matter to you.

So take another look at the domains in this chapter and hone in on those you identified as important. Take some time to visualize what you want to be about in each of those areas and what it would look like if you were living your life that way. And remember, this is about you, you, you! Do this exercise as if nobody will know what you come up with, and follow your heart. Really make an effort to come up with statements that are rooted in your experience.

If you find this hard, you're not alone. If it's hard because you're unsure what a domain is about, go back and reflect on the questions we pose within each area. If it's hard because you've never given this much thought, that's okay too. Be patient and take your time with it. Or it may be hard because thinking of intentions brings to mind what you've failed to do or regret having done. That can be painful, but again, you're not alone; everyone experiences this. Just remember that many worthwhile things in life are hard. This is one of them. You can do it.

In a minute, we'll ask you to write down an intention for each self-growth area that you consider important. Before you start writing, close your eyes and take a moment to visualize what it would be like for you to move in the direction that matters to you. Do this for each important domain. What do you see yourself doing? How does it feel to follow your heart and do something positive for yourself? Once you have it, put it into words as an intention.

When you're ready, go ahead and write your intentions below. If you need more space, use a separate piece of paper. And if you come up with more than one intention for any of the domains, that's great. Just write them down. As you write your intentions, listen to your gut—and also just notice how your mind might try to censor what you come up with, filling your head with thoughts like "Oh, that's far too difficult," "I'll never be able to do this," or "That's too self-indulgent."

Domain: _____

Intention: _____

_____

_____

Domain: _____

Intention: _____

_____

_____

Domain: _____

Intention: _____

_____

_____

To get a sense of how this might look, let's go back and see what Henry, the high school teacher and musician, came up with. He identified two self-growth domains as being important to him: The first was physical self-care and health, and the second was creativity. His health intention was to stay fit. In the realm of creativity, he wrote that he wanted to live a life filled with music, and then came up with two more specific intentions in this area: He wanted to play his guitar as much and as well as he possibly could, and he also wanted to learn as much as he could about classical music by both studying it and listening to it.

If you examine Henry's intentions, you'll see that these are things he'll never be able to complete as long as he's alive. There's always more to do. That's the true spirit of a valued intention.

Why Connecting with Your Self-Growth Values Matters

In this chapter and chapter 2, you've learned that knowing what matters is critical to creating a life of meaning and vitality. And this work has to start with you as a human being. We've said that values reflect the pristine in you, but that unspoiled part of you tends to get muddied with judgments and pain. It's like seeing a wild rose in bloom. Call it anything you wish, but the rose is still a rose. There's not a single rose—nor anything else for that matter—that comes into this world ugly and undesirable, or beautiful and irresistible. Our minds are what make it so. Values are pristine in that sense. They just are.

Values are the compass that can help you steer through life without losing your bearings. When you come to a crossroad, your values can help point you in the right direction. They can also help guide you in prioritizing how you spend your precious time. All of us face such choices each day, and often many times in a day. Some are big choices (Do I continue to work, or do I retire early so I can devote my time to leisure and creativity?), and others are seemingly small by comparison (Do I spend time writing an e-mail to a long-lost friend, or do I go for a run?).

Start connecting with your self-growth values. Keep them in the back of your mind, and reflect on them. Bring them to mind when you feel like you're slipping into doing what others expect or say you should do, or at times when you feel bogged down by activities that are far from your core. This will help you live out *your* dreams. It will also help you when you must choose between several valued directions. Learning how to prioritize and choose is covered in chapter 6.

None of us can add more hours to the day, but we can add more values and valued living to the day by thinking carefully about how we're using our time, and by giving minutes to our values as often as we can.

Chapter 4

Finding Meaning by Serving Others

We cannot live for ourselves alone. Our lives are connected by a thousand invisible threads, and along these sympathetic fibers, our actions run as causes and return to us as results.

—Herman Melville

A person starts to live when he can live outside himself.

—Albert Einstein

Life's most urgent question is: What are you doing for others?

—Martin Luther King Jr.

Service entails a shift in consciousness—a recognition that we are part of something larger than ourselves, that we have a role to play in the great circle of life, and that we can act to make a difference in the lives of others.

All of us live in interdependency. This is true even when you find yourself alone. The clothes you wear, the shoes on your feet, the food on your plate, and the roof over your head are there because of the actions of someone else—often many people, mostly faceless and nameless to us. We all serve each other. And yet it's easy to lose sight of this simple truth.

Why Does It Seem So Hard to Serve?

For some reason, we often seem to find the idea of service daunting. We think of it as a herculean task, best left to those with more time, money, skill, or resources. Even if we don't get stuck in feeling subpar, we may think that service belongs to the saints among us. These are all myths.

Service is something we all do. Saint and sinner, rich and poor, young and old alike—all can act in service. Nobody has a special corner on the service market. We all do it routinely anyway, mostly unconsciously and without much awareness that we're doing it.

That said, a number of factors conspire against our connection with other human beings. That sense of disconnect undermines our capacity to serve. When we're disconnected, we feel alone. And when we feel alone, we tend to shut down and focus on our own needs and survival. That self-focus limits our ability to see beyond our own situation, an ability we need if we are to reach out to others. It also stands in the way of benefiting, in kind, from what others could share with us.

Still, people are reaching out, and increasingly with newer forms of communication technology and social media. Many people are plugged in to one or more devices almost continuously. In mere seconds, we can go online and expand our social network, updating others on our status and creating virtual friendships, grudges, and love affairs. In this online world, we spend a lot of time commenting on what we think, have done, or are about to do. And then we remark on the social commentary others offer about their lives. In all of this, we're limited to a virtual world that draws on only two of our five senses—sight and sound. These are the same senses at work when you watch TV.

This communication technology is incredibly seductive and taps a basic human need for connection with other human beings. But there's a dark side to all of this. Virtual connection can pull us out of our lives and the grist of living that comes from real-world, hands-on interaction with other human beings. An emoticon smile or tear or an iconic hug can't substitute for emotional expression as it unfolds in a face-to-face interaction with another person. Service and genuine human connection flow from such hands-on experiences. They touch us with all five of our senses, and in a way that transcends the exchange of words, images, and ideas. It's no wonder then that many people are feeling more connected now than ever before, and also more disconnected. Something is missing.

Many people also feel powerless to create change. We see places where we want to act and make a difference, but then we tend to minimize our potential to make a difference. The problems just seem too insurmountable, and even too much to bear. Thinking that we have to do more, have more, or be something other than what we are in order to make a significant difference in this world just adds weight to the sense of paralysis that so many people feel. With that, "I can make a difference" morphs into "How could I ever make a difference?" This stops us in our tracks.

Time is a precious commodity too. Millions of people are working harder, yet feel as though they have less to show for it. Overscheduled and overburdened are common buzzwords, leaving many people feeling like there isn't time or space for more activities, even if "more" means doing what matters or serving others. This can leave us feeling like we're mired in the routines of life, and with a sense that we just don't have anything more to give. There's so little time to pause and appreciate what we have and what we have to offer.

What we look like, how we dress, where we live, the cars we drive, and the jobs we hold spotlight our individuality, while also punctuating our differences. That also creates a sense of disconnection and aloneness. And as if all of this weren't enough, each of us has a mind that can turn just about anything into pain and despair. So we harden and close in on ourselves. Our connections with others evaporate and we feel detached, isolated, and alone.

All of this (and more) works together to feed what Buddhists call the monkey mind, what psychologists call habits, and what most people think of as distractions, busyness, and routines. This mode of mind keeps us jumping from one thought or activity to the next, always one step ahead of ourselves, on the move, and focused on our own needs and desires. It is, in a way, both self-serving and self-preserving. Either way, it creates an illusion of separation or disconnection that simply isn't so.

Pausing and noticing our ties with the larger whole of humanity is a powerful way to tame the monkey mind. And when we pause, we can see that we are not so alone. Each of us has a role to play. Our actions create ripples that influence other human beings, and each of us is touched by the ripples created by others.

The Ripple Effect

In his book *Dangerous Undertaking: The Search for Transformation*, James Harlow Brown describes the ripple effect something like this: Imagine that you're sitting by a pond, contemplating. You catch a glimpse of a frog jumping into the pond and notice how the ripples spread out across the surface. You watch more intently and realize that the surface is alive with other sources of movement.

You see insects touching the water and causing tiny ripples. A swallow swoops down and grazes the surface as it catches a bug. A light breeze gently brushes your cheek and then creates more ripples as it washes over the pond. As you continue to watch, you see that all of these ripples interact, creating complex and ever-changing patterns on the surface of the pond.

And then you arrive at an important insight: Each event was writing its unique pattern on the water, and the ripples continued to reverberate long after the event occurred. As it turns out, this is how the world works too. We make ripples every moment of our lives, and these ripples create the future.

If you allow yourself to sink into that a bit, you may notice that you're watching the pond from a distance, as if you have no role to play. But you do. In the real world, there's no bank to sit on, and few of us have that luxury anyway. You're right in the pond of life, along with everyone else on this planet. Your actions are the epicenter for your impact on the world. Ripples flow outward from that epicenter, to combine and interact with the ripples fashioned by others.

This is an important insight too, and when you follow it, it will naturally pull you out of yourself and bring you into contact with this simple truth: All of us are constantly creating patterns and influencing one another, because we're all in the same pond. Seeing ourselves as together in the "pond of life" is a shift in thinking that draws our attention to the immediate and lasting impact of our behavior on other human beings.

Anjali Desai, part owner of the Seva Cafe in India, wanted to explore this ripple effect. She set out to cultivate a spirit of service by asking each of her customers to make a donation toward the next person's meal. No bill is left at the table; diners receive only a simple request to give from the heart. Those who follow experience the generosity of those who came before, yet do not know the source. Devoted to the principle "Think globally, act locally," Anjali's communal experiment in giving reminds us that our actions, however small, affect someone or something else. We are all interconnected in some way.

The Spirit of Service

Service is fundamentally an act of giving of oneself with no strings attached. This is not an "I do for you, you do for me" quid pro quo type of arrangement. When you serve, you discover and develop your natural talents and interests and use them to reach out to others and to the world.

Nobody else can do that for you, just as nobody else can live your life for you. You do it just because service matters to you, and *only you can do it*. This involves a shift from self- to other-awareness and from self- to other-responsibility. Both shifts put you in touch with the greater part of humanity.

Service also does more than connect us with one another. It helps us find meaning and purpose in our lives. In a way, it allows us to share and express our self-growth values with others. So if you value teaching, you share knowledge and help others grow. An act of kindness or a smile may brighten someone else's dark moment. Or a song that flows from your creative passions may enrich someone's life. Sharing your self-growth values creates powerful ripples.

Beyond that, the act of sharing the expression of your values is empowering, and a gift to yourself and others. As you manifest your values, you add something to your life and to the lives of those you contact. This explains the saying that what you give, you often get back tenfold. This giving and receiving unfolds like a dance. It isn't something we control; it evolves more or less on its own.

Helping others is also like this. People are naturally drawn to help one another. Just don't limit your service to situations where help is needed or something needs to be fixed. There's good reason for this. Helping can be seen as operating from a stance of inequality, not a relationship between equals. In this way, helping works because you perceive yourself to have something that someone else lacks.

Fixing can be like that too—the fixer is whole and the person who seems in need of fixing is broken or deficient. You're operating from abundance, while those you help are operating from impoverishment or deprivation. People sense this inequality, and that tends to magnify differences and diminish dignity, worth, and wholeness. Circumstances may be deficient, but not people.

There will be times and situations when you don't feel strong, or when you're lacking in energy, motivation, or resources. However, it's important to serve then too. If you serve only during times of abundance, you limit your capacity to serve. You'll also limit your capacity to live your life. Reread the first sentence of this paragraph to see why.

It may seem like semantics, but it's useful to recast giving and helping as service. Service doesn't operate from a position of strength or plenty. It flows forth from your core—from your heart and soul. It manifests as you draw upon your unique talents and experiences and connect with others just as you would with yourself.

You can serve from a position of strength or weakness, from darkness or light, and with your wounds and limitations. Your wholeness as a human being serves the wholeness in others and the great circle of life. This is why service is fundamentally a relationship between equals.

This also helps underscore how true giving goes beyond material things. Often the most meaningful things we can give and receive cost nothing in a monetary sense: a smile, a helping hand, a kind word, a thank-you, an act of generosity, a moment of appreciation or love, a hug, or even a handshake.

If you've ever been there for someone in need, provided a listening ear, or reached out to help someone, you've created ripples in service to another human being. Service is intimately woven into the fabric of life, giving us strength and purpose while also helping us feel not so alone in this world.

There are many examples of this spirit of service, some astonishing and profound. Mother Teresa, for instance, chose a life of poverty while serving the poorest of the poor on the streets of Calcutta. She's described as a saint, but what she gave in service is something each of us has within us: compassion, a word of encouragement, an expression of hope, or a loving touch. She understood that ordinary gifts can be used in extraordinary ways.

Many children recognize this too. Kids have a knack for thinking beyond themselves. Stephanie, an eight-year-old, is a good example. After reading a newspaper article about an injured baby manatee, she decided that she wanted to do something. She began making manatee pins. She sold them to family and friends to raise money for the cause, and to raise public awareness.

Other kids got wind of her efforts and were inspired by what she was doing. They wanted to get involved too. The result is a nonprofit called Kids Making a Difference, an organization run by kids, for kids. Its mission is to bring youth together to create positive change in their communities and the world.

Sometimes the opportunity to serve is thrust upon us. James, a healthy seventy-five-year-old empty nester, retired after a very successful twenty-five-year run as owner of a mom-and-pop real estate business. He and his wife had sacrificed a great deal for the family and the business, and both were looking forward to spending their golden years traveling, visiting their grandchildren, and enjoying life. Within a period of a few short months, life dealt both of them an unexpected blow.

James watched his wife's good health deteriorate rapidly, leaving her connected to a catheter, wearing a diaper, and requiring a walker to get around. And after multiple tests, consultations, and doctor's visits, they learned that she had developed a rare and mysterious neurological condition with no known cure. With that, James sensed his dreams fading too.

In an odd and somewhat twisted way, this painful turn of events provided James with an opportunity—a call to serve his wife. He felt that pull in his gut and heart, and this strengthened his sense of duty and responsibility to her. The illness robbed them of an *idea* of a future, but not what both of them valued most: a future that reflects and honors their relationship and love for one another.

The bottom line is that service is something we all do. It just needs to emerge from our core, our epicenter of impact in this world.

Finding Your Service Epicenter

The location of your service epicenter is determined by your talents, passions, and values. Like everyone, you have a unique and special set of talents: the things you're particularly good at. The same is true of your passions: the things that tug at your heart, enliven your spirit, or pull at your sense of resolve, justice, and responsibility. The directions in which you take these talents and passions are informed by your values. Together, your talents, passions, and values form a nexus that adds richness to your life and meaning to your acts of service.

In just a bit, we provide several exercises to help you discover some of your talents and passions. Later, we'll help you explore and clarify your service values.

At this point, we recommend that you get a sheet of paper and divide it into four columns. Label the first column "my self-growth values," the second "my talents," the third "my passions," and the fourth "my impact on others." Copy your self-growth values into the first column, and then as you continue reading, fill in the remaining columns. If you don't have time right now to put this down on paper, that's okay. You can return to this activity later on.

Your Talents

Your mind might tell you otherwise, but you do have talents. Some may have required years of work to develop, while others seem to flow naturally from your core. These talents are your unique set of attributes, skills, and abilities. When you manifest them, others sense your talents in what you do. And if you're fortunate enough, you may have heard people comment on them from time to time.

Take a moment to reflect on each of your self-growth values in terms of your unique talents and interests. What natural abilities do you have in each area? Think of things that you're good at or excel at, that you enjoy doing, or that seem to cry out for expression. Some may be underdeveloped; others have been with you since childhood. And if your mind tells you that you don't have any talents in a certain area, simply thank your mind for that thought and return to the exercise.

You may have a knack for leading others, teaching and sharing what you know, bringing people together, or getting things done. You may be good with finances, cooking, sports, outdoor activities, or technology. You may have a natural ability to be attentive to your needs and those of others, to listen, to brighten a dark moment, to rise to a challenge, or to face hardship and adversity. You may share easily and give freely, wherever you find yourself. As you reflect, you're likely to discover that you have many talents. When you're ready, jot down whatever talents you come up with for each of the self-growth values you listed on your piece of paper. There's no right or wrong with this.

Once you've written down talents for each of your self-growth values, look for common themes. Perhaps you're good at organizing, planning, and keeping commitments. Maybe you're creative, whether with problem solving, writing, music, singing, dance, or other forms of artistic expression. You may have talents for working with your hands, or your talents may be expressed through your intellectual abilities.

If you're having trouble with this exercise, think back in time, perhaps to a "happy" period in your childhood. Imagine that you're watching yourself as a young child, full of promise and potential, just as a parent, friend, or caregiver might do. You see yourself in this little child, and in what that child brings to the world. Think of how you'd comment on that child's talents, interests, and abilities. What does he or she enjoy doing? What is this child good at? Where does he or she seem to thrive? And if you had a crystal ball and could make a prediction based on what you see, what would you say about the future talents of this child? Don't overthink it. Just jot down whatever you come up with.

Talents are important because they're something you can develop and share with others. Plus, acting on your talents often brings a sense of personal satisfaction, meaning, and purpose. So when you develop and share your talents, you're both enriching your life and giving others a gift of yourself. Expressing your talents serves others and creates ripples on the pond.

Your Passions

It's common for people to offer advice along the lines of "Do something that you're passionate about." They're right. Far too many of us shuffle through life doing things that we don't feel strongly about, whether at work, in relationships, or in the myriad of obligations and have-tos that seem to fill our days. Discovering your passions is important. It will add zest to your life and help give you direction and a sense of purpose in serving yourself and others.

Our passions are reflected in things that raise our spirits, tug at our hearts, or ratchet up our sense of resolve. When we experience and live our passions, they can make us feel more alive and motivate us to act on our values and serve others. Still, many people struggle to identify what they feel passionate about. We tend to be much better at knowing what we seem to lack, desire, or want more of in life.

As odd as it may sound, this sense that something is missing can be an important clue to your passions. Before going into this more deeply, consider whether you feel that you lack something in your life right now. If so, can you give it a name? Don't do this as an intellectual exercise. Sink into it with your heart and gut. What's missing as you reflect on each of your self-growth values? Just make a note of what shows up for you.

The exercises below will take you into this process of discovery a bit more deeply. Each is meant to help you further connect with your passions as you consider your life and your service to yourself and others.

A Trip to a Deserted Island

Go back to your self-growth values and review them all. Now imagine that you can have all of them—without limits! Imagine that you're taking them with you on a trip to a deserted island, where you'll be for some time. You load your boat with your self-growth values and head out to sea. Before reading on, take out a piece of paper and create a ship's manifest—a list of the self-growth values that you packed on board.

As you head toward the island, you notice that your boat is at risk of taking on water from the weight of everything you brought along. You'll need to toss one of your values overboard. Have a good look at your inventory. Which value would you toss away? Once you've decided, go ahead and cross it off your list.

Turns out, that wasn't quite enough. You're still in danger of sinking. You'll have to pick another value to cast overboard. Which one will you choose? Go ahead and select it, then cross it off your manifest. Your boat is lighter, but you're still taking on some water. You'll need to select another value to toss away. Go ahead and do that.

Continue with this exercise until you're down to one of your self-growth values. This will be the only value you can take with you if you're to make it to the island alive. Which one did you choose? And why did you choose it? Look to your heart and gut and see if there's something in that value that you feel strongly about. This is one of your passions.

If You Could Grant Only One Wish

Imagine someone very special to you. Bring this person to mind as vividly as you can. Once you do, imagine that you could grant this person a wish and it would come true. This wish is something that ought to have some durability to it. Be mindful that if you wish for something emotional or a state of mind, those tend to be ephemeral and probably won't last long. Think carefully. You have only one wish. Make it something that will last. What would it be? Take a moment and sink into what you'd wish for this special person. The only rule is that you can't wish for money or things—or more wishes!

Now pause and reflect on what you came up with. Was your wish something that you would also wish for yourself and for other human beings? Is it something that you feel strongly about or that pulls at your heartstrings? It could also be something that you seem to lack or perhaps want more of in your life.

When Janet did this exercise, she imagined her oldest daughter, Tina, who suffers from cerebral palsy. Trapped in a wheelchair, Tina was often the target of attention, but for all the wrong reasons: an object of pity, idle curiosity, or scorn. Janet, knowing that Tina's disease has no known cure, wished this for her daughter: "a whole life—a life where she would not be so alone, a life filled with caring and loving relationships."

When Janet stepped back, she sensed that this was something she wanted desperately for herself too. For many years, she had suffered from a sense of being the outcast—the brainy kid and the target of bad jokes and bullying in school. She carried this with her into her adult years. Her wish for her daughter was a wish for herself and something that she felt deeply about.

What Tugs at Your Heart?

There are few people who enjoy crying, and yet tears provide a window into what you truly care about. Janet felt tears well up each time she imagined her daughter growing up alone, isolated, and cloistered in assisted living. It tore her heart out to think of that future, and her pain moved her to act. Janet became an advocate for her daughter and others suffering from cerebral palsy. This became her passion.

Your pain can teach you something about what you care about. A good place to start is by taking a deep look into your own life. Where have you suffered? Did the actions of other people contribute to that suffering? What was it that they did? What was it that they seemingly robbed you of?

Now see if you can imagine what you would need to restore your sense of wholeness, dignity, and justice. If you fear suffering in the future, what form does that take? Allow yourself to linger with these questions for a bit, and jot down whatever you come up with.

Now expand your horizons to the world around you. Imagine seeing others go through pain and suffering similar to your own. You might imagine seeing this via the media, television, or movies, in your daily life, or in relationships with others who are important to you.

When you see others experiencing your suffering, how does that affect you? Does it tug at your heart? Do you feel a pull, a compulsion to act or defend, to reach out to alleviate that suffering, to right the wrongs, or to create peace? This is important, so take some time with it.

Your pain will often point to your passions, and to where you feel most compelled to reach out to others in service. Just be careful.

It's very easy for a sense of justice and resolve to morph into anger, and this can take you down a path that's ultimately hurtful, to you and to others.

So, don't let your anger do the work for you. Anger can be used for good or for ill. The same is true of just about any emotion, even happiness. Passions ought to point you in a heartfelt direction, but you still need to decide whether and how to act.

Exploring Your Service Values

Your service values are inherently social, of course, but they flow from your self-growth values. This is one reason we started with self-growth values: because your life and your potential impact on others pivot on you taking care of your own place in the pond. Now it's time to expand the list of valued domains you started in the previous chapter by considering other dimensions of life that more directly involve your relationships with other people.

Go through this exercise as you did before when considering your self-growth values. As you read the descriptions of each domain below, ask yourself, "Is this area important to me?" We know that we're leaving out any middle ground here, but that's for a reason. We'd like you to drawn a line in the sand with these areas when it comes to their importance for you. Anything else, like "kind of important," "moderately important," and so on, would be conditional. When people get conditional about their values, they tend to end up on the fence, going nowhere, particularly when things get difficult. And being stuck on a fence isn't good as far as your life is concerned.

As you consider this, be mindful that importance doesn't necessarily mean this part of your life is currently well developed. For instance, when Mary, a single, middle-aged office clerk went through this exercise, she wasn't involved in an intimate relationship and hadn't started a family. Still, she rated the domains of family and intimate relationships as very important in her life. Later on, when she was married and her first child was on the way, she returned to this exercise and expanded upon it. The key is to look at this as a process—your life circumstances and experiences may change, but what you care about in your gut tends not to change in dramatic ways.

If you say "yes" to an area, meaning that it's important to you, also rate how satisfied you are with your life in this area right now, again using a scale from 0 to 2 where 0 means not at all satisfied with your life in this area, 1 means you're moderately satisfied, and 2 means you're very satisfied. As before, we've posed some questions to help you explore these areas, along with examples of intentions people have made in each area. Later on, we'll help you develop some valued intentions in the domains that are important to you.

Family

This domain covers all aspects of family life, with a focus on your relationships with your partner or spouse, children, siblings, parents, and other relatives. Take a moment now to consider your family life.

Are your family bonds important to you? Do they give you a sense of meaning and purpose? What sort of partner would you like to be in an intimate relationship? Consider also your role as a caregiver and parent, and reflect on what kind of parent you wish to be. What kind of relationship do you want to have with your parents or siblings? Are these roles and relationships important to you, and if so, how?

Be mindful of your passions and talents in this area too. What do you bring to this domain, and what do you feel strongly about in this area? Also think about whether there's anything missing from your life in this area.

Family is an area of deep importance to Catherine, a recently retired paralegal and also a mother and grandmother. As she considered her intentions, she offered this: "My family is my lifeblood. I would like to be there for my grandchildren so that they know me and how much I love them and want the best for them. I never had that kind of relationship growing up. My grandparents were distant. I'd like to be a special part of their lives and share with them—what I know, but mostly my love and support."

Stewart and his wife recently married and are now thinking about their future, including starting a family. He also values family greatly and described his intentions this way: "I want to be a loving spouse and a good dad. I'd like to show that with my wife by listening to her and being attentive, loving, and strong in good times and bad. I want to show appreciation and gratitude and share that with my wife, and someday, hopefully, my kids."

Yes   No   Is this area important to you? (Circle one.)

0   1   2   If it's important, how satisfied are you with your
                 life in this area right now? (Circle one.)

Friendships and Other Social Relationships

While we're all social creatures, there's a lot of variation in what we value in the realm of social relationships and their depth and scope. Some people value knowing many people, even if they don't know any of them particularly well. Others place a premium on having a few close friendships. Still others prefer a mix of friendships, some with depth and others relatively shallow. And then there are people who prefer to be alone.

Depth relates to degree of intimacy, whether emotional, spiritual, or intellectual. So think about the importance and quality of your social life. Are social bonds important to you? What kind of relationships would you like to have? What personal qualities would you like to develop in and through your relationships? How would you interact with your friends if you were the "ideal you" with them?

Where would you like to create ripples of service in your friendships and other social relationships? Again, also give some thought to your talents and passions, and to what might currently be missing in this area.

Ben, a twenty-four-year-old musician, has hundreds of friends, not counting those on Facebook. When he looked at his intentions in this area, he shared this: "I just love meeting new people. I'd like to be the kind of person who is willing to share myself, even if I know that I'll probably never see someone again. I want people to feel like they can be real with me, and to have that, I strive to be real, open, and honest with my friends and people I meet. I want people to know that they can trust me and count on me."

Sherry, a married empty nester, had just celebrated her fiftieth birthday with her husband and some close friends. When thinking about her intentions in terms of social relationships, she shared this with us: "I've never been someone who's had lots of friends. My husband is my best friend, and behind him I have a handful of women and a few men who I consider my dear friends. I want to be someone who my friends can count on. I'd do anything for them, and I think they'd do the same for me. I want to be available, kind, open, giving of myself, and a rock in their lives."

Yes   No   Is this area important to you? (Circle one.)

0   1   2   If it's important, how satisfied are you with your life in this area right now? (Circle one.)

Community and Volunteerism

We all belong to a community of some sort. You can think of this area broadly or more narrowly, from being a citizen of a country or state to being involved in your town or neighborhood to the role you play in a social group, your workplace, a religious or secular group, or an organization. It's likely that you feel a connection with community on many of these levels. And it's also likely that you place varying degrees of importance on giving back in terms of your time, talents, and resources.

With all of this in mind, is being part of a community—something larger than yourself—important to you? Do you care about giving back or making a difference in the lives of others in your community? What kind of person do you want to be at whatever level you find yourself? How would you like to share your talents and passions in your community? What pulls at your heart here?

Look to see if sharing, helping, or reaching out is important to you, and if so, how you might express that. Also consider if you feel that anything is currently missing in this area of your life.

By most standards, Theresa has enough personal wealth to support a small developing country. Yet for her, community involvement means more than writing a check. She expressed it this way: "So many people think that money will solve the problems in our world. Sure, it can help. But what I want to do is get out in the world and give back with my sweat, time, and heart. I want to be someone who reaches out and takes action. I want to get in the trenches and play a part in making my world a better place. Community service is something I make time for. It pulls me out of myself, helps me grow, and leaves me feeling connected to other people and more alive."

Margaret, a college student working two jobs to pay her way, described her intentions like this: "For me, service is more than helping others. It's about being able to immerse myself in the culture of the service and the people. I feel humbled when I give of my time volunteering, and I take pride in giving back, whether at work, on campus, or in my local community. I want to be someone who never turns a blind eye on other people. I want to reach out and give, even when it feels like I have nothing to give."

Yes   No   Is this area important to you? (Circle one.)

0   1   2   If it's important, how satisfied are you with your life in this area right now? (Circle one.)

The Environment and Nature

Taking care of the environment is on the minds of many, and there are many ways to do that. You can also think of environment more broadly, as anywhere you might be, like at school, at work, at home, shopping, and so on. So, as you think about environment and nature on your own terms, consider some of these questions.

Is serving the planet important to you? For instance, do you enjoy taking care of your natural surroundings? Beyond things like recycling or conserving energy or water, this could include landscaping, planting a tree, or caring for a garden, or it might mean attending to your home or work space. Maybe you try to walk or bicycle whenever possible to cut down on your carbon footprint, or maybe you enjoy being outdoors in nature and sharing that experience with others. Enjoyment of the natural world can take many forms: hiking, camping, hunting, fishing, rock climbing, sailing, relaxing on the beach—the list goes on and on. Maybe you simply like to commune with nature in a contemplative way.

Pause here to consider what you care about in the environment or nature. How would you like to contribute to your environment? What sort of environments would you like to create at home, in your family, at work, or wherever you might find yourself? What environments would you like to spend more time in? Also consider how you'd like to use your natural talents and passions to influence your environment, and whether anything is missing in this area of life at this time.

Sean, a local guide in the Adirondack Park of New York, has an unbending love of nature. He described his intentions like this: "I spend most of my days outdoors and lead people on hikes and an occasional fly-fishing excursion to a remote pond. Many people don't get to see what I see, and I love sharing that with them. I also want them to develop a deeper appreciation for our natural world. So I spend a good amount of time teaching people about plants, animals, conservation, and geology during the trips. Even though I've taken the same hikes or fishing trips hundreds of times, when I bring a client along it always seems like the very first time for me. I want people to sense my passion and maybe grow in their love for the outdoors."

John, a teacher at a local college, reflected long and hard about his intentions in this area and came up with this: "Don't get me wrong, I love the outdoors, but here I'm thinking about the kind of environment I'd like to have in the classroom with my students. I teach very large classes and work hard to create an environment where students can speak and be heard. I want to be approachable, and so I work to get to know each student as best I can. It matters to me that each student knows that I care, and I'm guided by the credo 'Teach unto others as you would want to be taught.' I strive to show my love of learning and hope to inspire students to be lifelong learners."

Yes No   Is this area important to you? (Circle one.)

0 1 2   If it's important, how satisfied are you with your
               life in this area right now? (Circle one.)

The Golden Rule

Most people have heard of the golden rule: Do unto others as you would have them do unto you. Most societies and major religions have some version of this precept, yet people still find it hard to follow. At its core, the golden rule means taking care of others as you take care of yourself—or as you'd like to take care of yourself. You do that and show that by your actions. Good intentions just don't do the job of taking care of anyone, yourself included. So, how do you wish to treat yourself? Is being kind and compassionate toward yourself important? When you sense that others aren't kind or compassionate toward you, do you feel hurt, betrayed, or left with a sense of anger welling up inside?

When you see a lack of kindness, compassion, or goodwill, does it pull at your heart and compel you to reach out? This may be a clue that you value these qualities enough to express them with others.

So pause and reflect on how you'd like to "do unto" others—and yourself. What talents could you use to be more loving and compassionate toward yourself and others? How might you share this, even when you don't feel like it? Take some time with this one; we've never run across anyone who didn't want more of these basic qualities for himself or herself and for other people.

Doing for others was far from Tammy's mind for a very long time. She'd struggled with her self-confidence and self-worth for as long as she could remember and felt like she deserved very little. She sensed that something was missing in her life, and it turned out to be kindness and compassion for herself. Her intentions here were hard to express, but here's what she came up with: "I'm tired of being my own worst enemy. When I see people being treated badly, it tears me up inside. Why are people so cruel? Where's the kindness? I finally looked at that and realized that I never had learned how to be kind to myself, and that it wasn't my fault for not getting it when I was growing up. I want to be okay with being me and expressing myself as I am. I'd like people to know me, and I plan to be a bit gentler with myself and share that gentleness more with other people. That's what I want more than anything: to be an agent of good in the world."

Rick had had his fair share of hard knocks. His father was a workaholic, and his mother more or less cycled in and out of depression and in and out of the hospital. He grew up with an absent dad and a mother in need of constant care. From these experiences, Rick developed an inner strength and a yearning to reach out to others in need. His intentions boiled down to this: "I want to be available to others when they need me—and even when they don't really need much from me. It pulls at my heart to see people alone and suffering, for in them I see my myself. I want to be the kind of person who touches others in ways that lift them up."

Yes   No   Is this area important to you? (Circle one.)

0   1   2   If it's important, how satisfied are you with your
               life in this area right now? (Circle one.)

Developing Your Service-Oriented Intentions

It's time to pause, reflect a bit, and move from thoughts to intentions, as you did in chapter 3. Recall that an intention is simply a statement of how you'd like to live your life in an area that's important to you. It should capture the essence of what's most important to you in that area. Again, this isn't about what others want you to do or expect you to do, or even what you've told yourself you should or must do.

Remember that intentions differ from goals in that they have no end point; rather, they speak to how you want to live every day of your life in areas that matter to you. So take another look at the domains in this chapter and hone in on those you identified as important. Take some time to visualize what you want to be about in each of those areas and what it would look like if you were living your life that way. And remember, this is about you. Follow your heart, and do this exercise as if nobody will know what you come up with.

Take some time to focus on the service-oriented domains that are important to you. For each, begin by closing your eyes and taking a moment visualize what it would be like for you to move in the direction that matters to you in that domain. What do you see yourself doing?

Once you have the visualization in mind, go ahead and write it down as an intention in the spaces below. If you need more space, use a separate piece of paper. Again, more than one intention for any of the domains is fine. Just write them down.

Domain: _____

Intention: _____

_____

_____

Domain: _____

Intention: _____

_____

_____

Domain: _____

Intention: _____

_____

_____

The Three Pillars of Service

Your actions create your life and influence others. They are the pebbles that send ripples reverberating out across the pond. So it's important to move from thinking about doing something to actually doing something. Strip away all of the ideas about what service means, and you're left with three core aspects: awareness, choice, and action. These can be enacted by anyone. Let's have a look at each.

Simple Awareness

To find meaning in your acts of service, you'll need to develop awareness of two things: how you might serve others (your behavior and talents) and opportunities to serve (circumstances).

A simple way to increase your awareness is to slow things down from time to time and make a conscious effort to pay attention, on purpose, and right where you are. Notice what you and others are doing, and see if you can frame your actions and the actions of others in terms of serving.

To grow in your awareness, it can be helpful to ask yourself two questions: "How could I respond here to benefit myself *and* those around me?" and "How are the actions I'm taking right now possibly benefiting others?" Look to your values, talents, and passions to guide you.

Martha, a homemaker and mother of three, found herself faced with both questions while running around taking care of household chores. There were bag lunches to be made, laundry to do, and a host of things to attend to once the kids left for school. Feeling overwhelmed and tired, Martha took a slow, deep breath and brought her awareness to her role and how it benefited her family and her home.

She saw her children enjoying a wholesome lunch at school and wearing clean, fresh-smelling clothes, and thought of how this made them feel loved and special. She also noticed how her efforts with her kids and her home were part of something bigger than chores; she was manifesting her organizational talents, her creative talents, and her passions for the health and welfare of her children. She realized how important her role in the family was, and how it benefited her family. Ordinary and even mundane work around the house began to take on new meaning for her. Martha became aware of the pebbles she was dropping and the ripples she was creating.

Conscious Choice

There's no law in the universe that says you must act in service. You always have a choice to act or not. Each day you'll be faced with a myriad of opportunities to serve. Some will be thrust on you, pulling at your heart and resolve. We saw this with James, whose wife (and mother to one of us) was afflicted by a devastating illness soon after retirement. Other opportunities will flow from how you choose to live your life.

As you become more aware of these opportunities, you'll have to decide where you wish to drop your pebbles to make a difference. Small acts do add up. And many of the ripples you create may be unknown to you.

Also, be mindful that acts of service flow from you when you're living in a way that expresses your values. So the real question here is this: Where do you want to drop the pebble? Use your values as a guide. The ripples you create will fan out and influence others. This influence matters.

Taking Action

Service is all about action, or doing. People will know that you value service by what you manifest in the world—what you do with your mouth, hands, and feet. That's what they see about you, and what you'd see if you could watch yourself as if on a movie screen. So how do you wish to act in the realm of service values? What do you want to be known for? What kind of ripples do you wish to leave on the pond of life? Use your service intentions to guide you.

Expansive Reflection

Expansive reflection is about your connection to the greater human community and the world at large. It's a time to simply pause and reflect on the ripples you create each and every day. Imagine the possible impact of your actions on those in close proximity to you and on others who are far removed from you in time and space.

Imagine pouring yourself behind their eyes and into their hearts. See the difference you've made in them and how you're playing a part in the greater whole of humanity. Notice also the impacts of your acts of service on you, emotionally and spiritually, as you expand your sphere.

Expansive reflection begins at the point of impact, where you drop your pebbles in life. Then you broaden your gaze as the ripples cross and interact with the lives of other people. Notice how those ripples change others and change what they do, the pebbles they drop, and the ripples they create. On and on it goes. This is your legacy—your greater impact on the world.

Jamie did this while driving, with a simple act of letting a woman with a minivan full of kids into traffic during her rush-hour commute home. She'd had a rough day at work and wasn't feeling particularly giving. Traffic was snarled, and all Jamie wanted to do was get home. Yet she saw this woman trying to get into traffic and became aware of the opportunity to serve. She made a choice to do something and then took action by allowing the woman to merge into her lane. She dropped a pebble.

After that, she paused in a moment of expansive reflection. She imagined the impact of her gesture. She felt relief washing over the woman and how that eased the stress of driving a carload of screaming kids. Jamie went further to see the impact of that on the children, and imagined all of them making it to a special event on time, and how that made them happy. She went further and saw the kids sharing their stories with their father at the dinner table later that evening, and at school with friends the next day. This moment of expansive reflection put a smile on Jamie's face and filled her heart with warmth. It just felt good, whether her images were true or not.

Like a ripple expanding out, your actions in the spirit of service may continue to reverberate long after you drop the pebble. Expansive reflection provides you the opportunity to connect with this broader impact. And you can do it anytime, anywhere.

Making a Difference in the World

Most people dream of a better world but feel powerless to do anything about it. We forget we're all interconnected in some way. We forget that everyone has something to share. We miss that opportunities to serve are often right under our nose. As we get caught up in day-to-day life, we tend to miss that we're all creating ripples, influencing others and ourselves.

Service is your impact on this world—both immediate and lasting. When you serve, you're living your values by turning your intentions into actions and sharing your talents and passions with others. That's why you get something back when you act in the spirit of service. Your life expands and you gain the renewed sense of purpose and meaning that comes from being part of something larger than yourself. This is your lasting legacy.

Still, service can be hard. So many things can get in the way of living out our values and becoming aware of our impact on others. These barriers feed the illusion that we are alone in this world and have nothing to give, particularly during times of hardship, weakness, and personal pain. And worse, they can keep us from doing what matters. But these barriers are surmountable, and in chapters 7 through 10, we'll help you learn how to work with them.

Chapter 5

Life Purpose

The purpose of life is a life of purpose.

—Robert Byrne

The way you get meaning into your life is to devote yourself to loving others, devote yourself to your community around you, and devote yourself to creating something that gives you purpose and meaning.

—Mitch Albom

Efforts and courage are not enough without purpose and direction.

—John F. Kennedy

U p to this point in the book, you've explored self-growth and service values and how they link you with other human beings. There's one more step to take in the process of uncovering the values that matter most to you. This chapter offers a chance to examine your life purpose—the reason you're here, your most important work, the great challenge you keep returning to over the years.

Awakening to Your Life Purpose

Your life purpose probably isn't what you do for a living, nor is it likely to be entirely contained in such roles as parent, spouse, writer, or civic leader. Rather, life purpose runs like a thread or theme through the roles you play, the things you do, and the relationships you most care about.

Life purpose can even appear as a conflict, such as in situations where social forces, needs, or natural propensities pull you in one direction while a core value draws you in another. Or your life purpose may reveal itself in moments of calm, when you see your choices clearly and recognize the difference between your desires and the things that really matter—between what you do and what your mission truly is.

The obvious things about life—our interactions, our daily tasks, our recreation—don't always yield the truth about why we're here. But how we *respond* to each element in our life tapestry, how we navigate each option and possibility, provides hints about our core purpose.

As an example, let's consider some recent events in the life of Erica, a twenty-six-year-old nurse. After graduating and becoming an RN, she started work on a surgical ward. A year of shepherding her patients through post-op recovery was interesting and she learned a lot, but something was missing. Additional training in pediatric nursing allowed her to land a job at an outpatient pulmonary program for asthmatic children in Houston.

Then Erica's grandmother, Mildred, had a stroke and had to move into a nursing home. Mildred lived in Chicago, and because no other family members remained in Illinois, Erica helped her grandmother move to a convalescent facility in Houston so she could visit frequently and monitor the quality of her care.

A year later, Erica saw a story in the *Houston Chronicle* about Bhutanese refugees who had been driven from their homeland and were now housed just a few miles from her. They needed help with assimilation and English as a second language. An hour later, Erica had signed up as a teacher.

While a common thread through all of Erica's decisions is caring for others, we must look deeper to find Erica's life purpose. What matters most to her is protecting vulnerable people (children, old folks, refugees). In fact, this core value drove her decision to leave post-op so she could serve kids with breathing disorders. It was a problem calling out to her heart for a resolution.

While Erica is unusual in her generosity, she's quite ordinary in her pursuit of a consistent life purpose. Most of us, if we carefully review key moments over the years, will find themes that point to our core purpose. Sometimes these are clearly recognized with only a moment's thought; in other cases they are opaque and perhaps seen more easily by others than by ourselves.

Barry, a retiring bookstore owner, was surprised by a speech in his honor at a service club luncheon. A longtime friend stood before the group and said, "Your whole life has been about getting people together for a common goal. It showed in how you gathered loyal employees with a passion for reading and talking about great books. It showed in how you got us to work together to start a literacy program. It showed in the Little League team you talked us into founding—and then coaching. It showed in countless barbeques in your backyard, where you sold us on one harebrained scheme after another. Remember the one where we had to slosh through the mudflats, pulling out old tires?"

That brought an explosion of laughter, and in that moment something was clear. Barry suddenly had the sense that his life had been about something—something both within and beyond the affection of friends and a feeling of having done well. He laughed and made a you-got-me gesture, but he could see that his life—from his earliest days—felt good and right when he found ways to join people.

As a last example, consider Jeff, a woodshop instructor at a technical college. His life's passion was learning things, the more challenging the better. Whether it was Japanese woodworking, guitar making, or the intricacies of sailing, he exhaustively studied each subject. Then he'd find someone to share those skills with, including a troop of Sea Scouts who sailed with him each Sunday. Friends joked that he didn't seem much interested in *making* guitars and furniture once he'd mastered the skills. What Jeff loved was taking on something new.

The Heart of Purpose

Notice that the stories of Erica, Barry, and Jeff have something in common: All three were naturally drawn to situations and events that were relevant to their life purpose, and all of them found they had much less passion for experiences that weren't as closely aligned with that purpose. In other words, what you find yourself wanting to do across many years and many types of situations is a strong indicator of life purpose.

Within all of that is a central element: We see a problem, something amiss, and we're passionate about working toward a solution. You'll know it in your gut when you see something missing in yourself or others. You may see social injustice or a lack of personal growth. You might respond to illness, mistreatment, or an opportunity to help. Perhaps disorganization, a need for leadership, a pull to bring people together, or the absence of love and compassion call out to you. Whatever it is, finding your purpose often comes back to solving a problem that plays over and over again as a recurring theme in your life, drawing you back and pulling at your heartstrings. You can't ignore it.

But there's more to finding your life purpose than looking back at situations that call out to you or discovering what you naturally enjoy. Choices that move us in the direction of a core value often require initiative in the face of obstacles. They may involve struggle or sacrifice.

Let's consider a few examples to make this clear. When Barry started the literacy program, he truly enjoyed getting folks fired up to work on it. But he had a wretched time finding a site for the program and raising funds. When he tried to lease a house for the project, people he considered friends pushed the city council to deny a zoning variance. What started out so gaily over beans and pork ribs became a battle, and it took all of his skills to finally launch the program.

The same kind of challenge played out with Walter, a brittle, difficult man who worked part-time as a book editor and hated it. He was also a talented composer, and the hours he spent writing music were his happiest times. He'd arranged his life so he could be at the piano much of every day.

Walter's wife, Katherine, who loved and supported him, had to bear his near-constant complaints about anything that interrupted his work. Although Walter loved her and his children, he didn't spend as much time with them as they would have liked. Often he was more drawn to his music than to his family. So he just composed tight, complex little melodies and then sent them off to high-profile publishers.

Walter may seem like a curmudgeon, but he had a soft spot or two. That softness came out in times of need. One of those difficult times involved his wife. Katherine took a bad fall off a ladder in their garage and injured her foot terribly. When Walter heard her cries for help, he sprang from his piano and rushed to her aid. He carried Katherine to the car, then took her to the hospital. She required surgery and was laid up for weeks.

During that ordeal, Walter temporarily abandoned his piano to care for her and took on the family duties that normally fell to her, including getting his oldest daughter, Alison, to and from softball practice. Walter made time for that and even lingered to watch Alison play—something he hadn't done before. As it turned out, Alison made the high school varsity softball team, and Walter became her biggest fan, never missing a game. Yes, he didn't like interruptions while he worked, but he was also willing to adjust to make clear that, when push came to shove, his creative musical passions didn't trump his family.

A life purpose doesn't diminish other people; it doesn't rob them of love and support. Rather it compels us to act, to work for something and toward something over and over again, and in many ways.

Living a life of purpose isn't easy. Clashes between values are common and can be quite tricky to resolve—enough so on both counts that chapter 6 is devoted to navigating values conflicts. The composer's life purpose was more than isolating himself with his piano. Perhaps it was to bring beauty to others or in some way enrich their lives. Or maybe he was responding to a problem he sensed: a world in need of melody and song.

One final thought about life purpose: It often entails a reciprocal relationship between learning and doing. We may need to learn compassion so that we can help others, yet the more we help, the deeper our compassion grows. We may need to learn leadership to effect change in the community, yet every campaign to improve the community may also increase leadership skills.

Finding Your Life Purpose

The rest of this chapter will help you uncover your life purpose. We've provided four exercises that will help you explore what pulls at you and where your purpose might lie. Each can provide insight. Try them all to discover which are most helpful to you.

The Tombstone Technique

In this exercise, you'll imagine looking back at your life from the time immediately following your death. Start by drawing the shape of a tombstone on a sheet of paper, then write your name at the top. Beneath your name, write the phrase "A person who..."

Now close your eyes and focus on your breathing for a minute or two. Just follow the breath as it enters your nostrils, flows down the back of your throat, and begins to expand your rib cage. Notice the feeling in your diaphragm as you release the breath and let go of the tension in your chest. Just keep your attention on your breathing until your mind slows down a little and your body grows more relaxed.

Now let yourself imagine that you've just died. Your tombstone is being carved with a single sentence that somehow captures what your life was about. This sentence expresses an ideal, a vision of what matters most to you. Don't worry if it isn't true about you right now; the intent is to make it true.

When you're ready, go ahead and write that sentence on your tombstone. This is your life, the core of what you're here to do. Look at the words and let them settle inside of you. Feel them in your heart and in your gut.

Now ask yourself this question: "How close or far am I from what I want my life to be about?" Notice what comes up. There may be images of things you wish you hadn't done, or images of things you'd do differently if you were given a chance. And amidst all of that, you'll see pictures of moments that are *exactly* how you want to live.

This is your opportunity to decide, clearly and consciously, the direction you want to take. You can start moving in that direction now. After all, the present moment is where all decisions happen, where you constantly choose to embrace, or not embrace, your life purpose.

Life Review

A life review is great way to zero in on your life purpose. It takes a little while, but it's time well spent. The idea is to look back at segments of your life to identify self-defining memories. These are recollections that stand out because they say something about your identity—what kind of person you strive to be.

Start the review process by dividing your personal history into eras: from birth to age ten, from age eleven to eighteen, from age nineteen to twenty-five, and in five-year periods thereafter. Use a separate piece of paper to review each era. Run a line down the middle of each page. Then, on one side, record up to five memories from that era that make you feel good about yourself. Focus on things you did or learned. On the other side of the page, note five memories that are disappointing, where you did something or noticed something about yourself that seems at odds with the person you want to be.

As you peer back in time, examine events in key relationships. Look at things you did to pursue goals and dreams. Recall your world at home or at work or school. Remember what you did creatively, and what you did for others. Also, think of books you read, movies you saw, or stories you heard that made an impact, set an example, or taught you something. As you reflect, also make contact with your talents and passions.

When you write a memory down, it isn't necessary to exhaustively describe the whole experience. Just identify the event in a sentence or two as a shorthand way to capture the essence of the memory.

If you can't come up with more than a few memories, particularly for your early life, don't worry. This process will still work, because each era of your life adds more information about what really matters to you. Just do your best to identify a few defining memories in every segment of your past.

Once you've written some memories for each era of your life, consolidate everything into unifying themes. Examine all of the memories that you feel good about, and reflect on what ties them together. Are there ways you've treated others, things you've done, or things you've learned that feel in alignment with a path or purpose?

Now look at the other memories—those that disappoint you and don't fit with who you want to be. What are the common elements here? What behaviors or ways of treating people seem to show up over and over?

Reflect on what you've learned from reviewing these two aspects of your life—what you feel good about and what disappoints you. And as you reflect, ask yourself these questions: "Who am I trying to be? What am I trying to learn? What am I trying to do?" Your answers will point directly to your life purpose.

As an example of this process, let's look at what Shelly, a thirty-six-year-old property manager, came up with. Here are her key memories for each era.

BIRTH TO AGE TEN	
Feel Good About Myself	**Disappointed in Myself**
• Helping Sara get home when she had her bike accident	• Making fun of the kid who wore hats with earflaps
• Finding my brother when he got lost	• Kicking my brother out of my room all the time
• Teaching my brother to fish	• Making fun of my brother for not knowing things
• Making friends with Rebecca (who was in a wheelchair)	• Fighting about toys
• Helping my father with chores when my brother was in the hospital	• Telling everyone my brother was crazy

| AGE ELEVEN TO EIGHTEEN ||
Feel Good About Myself	Disappointed in Myself
• *Being a counselor at summer camp and helping little kids when they were homesick* • *When our high school orchestra performed for the governor* • *Helping my brother adjust when he started high school and I was two years ahead of him* • *Reading Catcher in the Rye and really liking how Holden took care of Phoebe* • *Spending hours talking to Enid, who was struggling with anorexia*	• *Ignoring my dog after I got to high school* • *Things I said to Billy when I broke up with him* • *Being in a group that excluded several girls, who were very hurt by that* • *Making fun of my brother to my girlfriends* • *Refusing to let my brother hang around me and my friends*

AGE NINETEEN TO TWENTY-FIVE

Feel Good About Myself	Disappointed in Myself
• Graduating college, and all of us promising to stay close—which we did	• Being angry at my father because he always seemed concerned about my brother and not me
• Incredible sweetness and openness with Mark when we first met	• Told Jim he was weak and stupid in how he lived his life
• Starting Eating Disorders Awareness Week at college	• Not going to Cherie's wedding and getting defensive when she was upset
• Helping Mark, who had ADHD, learn how to organize and write essays	• Quitting soccer in a snit
• Writing a tune for Mark on the cello that he loved	• Not seeing my brother in the hospital

AGE TWENTY-SIX TO THIRTY

Feel Good About Myself	Disappointed in Myself
• *Helping Mark with his grad school application essays— after we broke up*	• *Not calling my father back when he left messages about my brother being in trouble*
• *Reading a book on bipolar disorder and realizing ways I could help my brother*	• *Splitting up with Mark—the anger*
• *Helping a homeless family with no credit get an apartment*	• *Sleeping with Len even though I knew he had a girlfriend*
• *Meeting the social worker who runs our homeless shelter and getting excited about helping*	• *Buying a Lexus instead of helping my family financially*
• *Spending a vacation week raising money for the shelter*	• *Bad-mouthing another real estate agent until they fired her*

AGE THIRTY TO THIRTY-SIX	
Feel Good About Myself	**Disappointed in Myself**
◆ *Helping the Merced family at the homeless shelter* ◆ *Paying three months rent for a mom and two kids at an apartment I managed* ◆ *Meeting Aaron and feeling like I could be myself with him* ◆ *Flying out to see Enid, whose divorce retriggered her eating disorder* ◆ *Getting my brother a new shrink and better meds*	◆ *Withdrawing and not being there for my brother after our father died* ◆ *After pressure from my boss, evicting the Sommers family* ◆ *Setting higher rents than some tenants could afford* ◆ *Not showing up for my brother's thirtieth birthday* ◆ *Selling my father's house instead of letting my brother live there*

Shelly's brother has bipolar disorder, which showed up as impulsive, angry outbursts during his childhood and as mania and depression in his adult years. For her entire life, Shelly often felt torn between caring for him and a strong desire to get away.

This review allowed her to see how her life purpose is defined by that struggle. She seeks to alleviate others' pain, and her disappointments in herself tend to revolve around times when she causes pain or difficulty for others. Over and over, her defining memories seem focused on helping or hurting, whether they involve her brother, her friends, or families at the homeless shelter.

Mindfulness-Based Journaling

Another way of uncovering your life purpose is mindfulness-based journaling. This technique involves paying attention to how your life unfolds and keeping a journal about what you notice. For the next two weeks, observe your life and be alert to any experiences that lead to feelings of well-being, rightness, significance, or admiration, then note them in your journal. We'll expand on that list a little to help give you a better idea of the types of experiences you're looking for:

- They create a sense of well-being or fulfillment.

- They feel somehow right and aligned with what you value.

- They stimulate a feeling of significance; a sense that this is important—pay attention!

- They lead you to feel admiration for someone else.

There are many categories of experience that might end up in your journal: conversations, a scene in a movie or TV program, something you read in the paper or a book, something you saw on the Internet, events in other people's lives, something you witnessed, something that touches you with its beauty, an activity or task, or even just a thought.

The easy part will be writing in your journal. The challenge in this process is mindful awareness: paying attention to the feelings of well-being, rightness, significance, or admiration as they show up in your life, and tuning in to the experiences that create these feelings. These experiences are a key to your passions and a window on your purpose in life. So be honest with yourself and don't censor anything that shows up. Your passions are something you need to be watching for all the time.

You don't have to write in your journal right at the moment when you have an experience. Making one entry each evening should be enough. But for the exercise to work, you have to be aware, *throughout the day*, of those feelings of well-being, rightness, significance, and admiration. You also need to notice what experiences triggered them. Once you've kept this journal for two weeks, review your entries to see if they point to a problem or issue that pulls at you for a resolution.

Here's an example of one week of a journal kept by Chuck, a forty-eight-year-old ornamental ironworker:

* *Wednesday: Coaching (middle school baseball). Felt good today. I like teaching the boys fundamentals. The infield drills, getting your glove down, getting your body in front of the ball. I like seeing them get it, seeing them stay with the ball and making a play.*

* *Thursday: Something I read in the obits. An old guy who'd trekked all over the world and gave free survival courses for backpackers. What to do if you get caught in a snowstorm or break a limb or an essential piece of gear, and so on. I like that feeling of giving away your hard-earned knowledge.*

* *Friday: Teaching one of the guys how to do tight scrollwork on this fence we're building. Also, my boy asking about how planes fly. Drawing him a cutout of a wing and showing him the principle of lift. He was so interested, and I felt like I was doing exactly what a dad is supposed to do.*

* *Saturday: Visited my mother-in-law. She was telling a story about her father showing her how to tap dance. He learned it from his uncle, who used to perform in bars. Even though nobody cared about tap dancing anymore, her dad passed it on to her, and they used to dance together. Now I'm thinking about time. How it connects one era to another as people pass on their knowledge. Showing how to do things that they learned. My wife asks what I've been writing about. I tell her. She says she's trying to pass on to our son how to be loving— how to pay attention and see what people feel and need.*

* *Sunday: In church there was a stupid sermon. And I looked across the rows of people and wondered why they were there. I felt they were there to learn something. Even if that idiot can't teach them, they came hoping to figure something out.*

- *Monday: Read that the old Bay Bridge will be demolished and thought about all of the work of those men hanging off the girders, working with hot rivets. What do they pass on when it's gone? What did they do that can last past an earthquake, past the decision to replace something? What do we have left after everything we make disappears?*

- *Tuesday: My son is afraid of the dark. He thinks something might take him while he's asleep. So I sit by his bed. He wants to know if it's okay to fall asleep. I tell him that the dark is just the sun being on the other side of the world, and nothing happens in the dark that doesn't happen in the light. He seems content with that and closes his eyes.*

You already know what Chuck's life purpose is. It shows up in nearly every entry. He's a teacher, passing on his skills and wisdom. It doesn't matter where that shows up—baseball, ironwork, or his son's fears—he's here to help people learn. That purposeful problem draws his interest and leads him to act again and again.

Life Lessons

Since life purpose can be just as much about learning as about doing, this exercise gives you a chance to explore personal strengths and qualities of character that you're striving to develop. There are two steps to the process.

Begin by writing down several virtues or personal qualities that you're trying to develop. These may be qualities you already possess but would like to strengthen, or they may be virtues you're trying to learn—for example, compassion, perseverance, acceptance, the ability to express or receive love, or the courage to face fear. You decide what's right for you.

For the next step, select the most important of these qualities, perhaps one that could help you accomplish key goals. Imagine that you already have this quality in abundance, then write about how your life would be different. What would you do differently with your friends, family, or colleagues?

Let's look at some of our previous examples to see how this exercise might contribute to gaining a fuller understanding of your purpose. Chuck, the ornamental ironworker, was clearly a teacher. But this exercise helped him realize that he's also trying to acquire patience and acceptance of people who are less competent. So in defining his life purpose, he puts both things together: "Learning to accept people for who they are, and teaching them what I know."

When Shelly, the property manager whose life review appears above, did this exercise, she realized that she wanted the strength to face pain—her own pain and that of others. In defining her life purpose, she combined learning and doing in this way: "Become a person who faces difficult things and helps people who are hurting."

Finding Your Purpose Matters

Now it's your turn to define your purpose. Use the exercises above to find words for what matters most to you, and remember that passion and purpose go hand in hand. When you've worked with all of the exercises for a while, try to distill your life purpose into one or two sentences. Write something pithy yet complete—the work you came here to do, the thing your life is most about.

Your sense of purpose may evolve over time. That's good. It means you're paying attention to how life changes and requires that you adapt. The important thing is to stay aware of opportunities to *act* on your life purpose. Opportunities to take actions that are guided by this core sense of what matters will show up in many arenas: relationships with friends and family, your work and your relationships with colleagues, involvement in your community, creative pursuits, opportunities for spiritual growth, and on and on.

Throughout life, keep asking yourself, "What would I do right now, in this situation, if I were guided by my life purpose? What would I be doing differently at this moment?" The more mindful you are of your life purpose, the greater its impact will be on your life and the lives of those you care about.

Chapter 6

Navigating Values Conflicts

Nothing is given to man on earth—struggle is built into the nature of life, and conflict is possible—the hero is the man who lets no obstacle prevent him from pursuing the values he has chosen.

—Andrew Bernstein

We have all been placed on this earth to discover our own path, and we will never be happy if we live someone else's idea of life.

—James Van Praagh

Commitment in the face of conflict produces character.

—Unknown

Your sense of what matters and your life purpose are starting to coalesce. If you lived in a vacuum, unencumbered by other life demands, you'd probably be able to just live out your dreams. But the world isn't like that.

We're all faced with a myriad of competing demands that threaten to keep us from going forward in ways that matter. We have to face choices, many of them difficult. And we're naturally drawn to situations that feel good but may not be so good for us in the grand scheme of things.

It's important to find a way to navigate the ups and downs of life so that you stay on course and don't become a rudderless ship, pushed by the wind and taken places you'd rather not go. You need a bearing to guide you when your values seem to collide with other demands, including other values. Our purpose in this chapter is to help you find your bearings when faced with values conflicts.

Being Pulled in Different Directions

Most people know what it's like to feel pulled in too many directions. Sometimes it's like being caught in a tug-of-war; we feel jerked back and forth and as though we're ultimately getting nowhere. This is an uncomfortable and difficult place to be. Life throws us these kinds of situations daily. They're hard to avoid.

The sense of being pulled in different directions flows from a conflict between two or more areas of life that are important to you. You want to say, "yes, yes, yes," but that can go only so far before something has to give. Saying yes to some things means saying no to others. That can hurt, especially when you're saying no to one or more of your deeply held values.

This tension can play out in countless ways. It might show up as a conflict between two values. Imagine that both family relationships and creative leisure time are important to you. Just as you're about to sit down and spend some time pursuing a hobby on a Saturday afternoon, your kids come in and ask you to take them to a soccer game. You can't be in both places at once, so you have to choose. Or maybe you have strong values about both supporting your partner and maintaining your health and fitness. It's a Sunday and you're about to go for a long run when your partner asks if you can help with some projects around the house. Because you value your health and fitness, giving up your run could leave you feeling uneasy.

We can also feel pulled between values and life demands. Noel, a forty-year-old mathematician, was all too familiar with this. He beamed as he told us about how he'd love to be a middle school math teacher. As he went on, the brightness slowly faded from his face. Then, after a small, somber pause, he said, "I can't do that. I'd have to leave my current job and say good-bye to a six-figure salary. My wife and kids love me, sure, but they'd never go for that." Noel found himself sandwiched between a job he wasn't crazy about and a six-figure lifestyle. With no easy way out, he felt squeezed and unfulfilled.

We have to make choices, many of them difficult. They're hard because we care. They're hard because values are involved. And they're also hard because how we choose, in small and large ways, determines the kind of life we create.

If we didn't care about what was at stake, none of this would matter. It might even be easy, like choosing between two outstretched hands that clearly hold nothing. But the choices in values conflicts aren't like that. The choice we make matters. It's about something precious to us. And often many things converge at once. It can seem like we're literally caught in a situation where every option seems like a poor choice.

Most people know what this is like, and you probably do too. It's hard being in a state of conflict—and even harder when the conflict is between your core values and social demands, economic necessities, or other needs of everyday life.

Financial demands can exert strong pressure on us. Like the whistle of a boiling teakettle, they seem very urgent, demanding our immediate attention and taking priority over everything else. This is exactly what happened to Noel.

How we navigate conflicts between the demands of daily life and our core values says much about the kind of life each of us will lead. If you're to examine this aspect of your life and consider making changes, it's important that you know something about how we humans tend to handle conflicting demands. We're predisposed to pay attention to the people, circumstances, or demands that seem most urgent, loudest, or most forceful.

Often, the demands that seem most urgent come from people we love or people who have some power over us. Much like the screech of car brakes or the roar of those hungry lions we talked about in chapter 1, these demands stop us in our tracks. They set off an alarm, and we feel we must respond. In that moment, we shift from our own interests and priorities to attending to the crisis at hand or whatever looms large on the horizon. Depending on how often this plays out, we can lose sight of facets of our lives that may be equally deserving of a voice, including our core values and life purpose.

If pain and hurt are allowed to run the show, the outcome is fairly predictable. People tend to feel burned-out, discontented, stressed, and unhappy. These feelings are a natural consequence of applying a great deal of effort and attention, but not in the right places. In the process of "doing more," it's easy to accomplish much less in terms of the things that truly matter. When we fail to attend to our own needs, we lose a sense of direction. Our values cry out for expression, but when they lack a "spokesperson," they're cast aside, suppressed, or forgotten.

And as if it isn't enough to feel bad about our lives being interrupted or even stalled by external pressures and demands, our minds often exacerbate the situation by offering up a seemingly unending stream of discouraging chatter. You may find yourself thinking, "Living out my values will never work. It's too hard." Or you may succumb to thoughts like "How can I do this? My life is already too hectic and difficult." This chatter may persuade you that it's okay to put off living your dreams with thoughts like "Someday I'll have more time to travel." Worse, it may call your values into question with thoughts like "Spirituality isn't that important anyway; it doesn't have any practical value" or "Self-growth is essentially self-serving, how selfish." This type of mind chatter can lead you to give up on your values altogether.

This can leave you feeling like life is a dead-end street. If this sounds like your situation, don't feel dispirited. There is a way out. It begins with learning to catch values conflicts early on, before they become oppressive and threaten to drown out your dreams. The next step is to develop strategies and techniques to prioritize your values so that you don't end up making choices that work against you in the long run.

Types of Values Conflicts and Clashes

The first thing you need to do when a values conflict occurs is to notice what's happening: What's in conflict, and which values are involved? Identifying the value or values at stake is important, because conflict can feel overwhelming, and that's an uncomfortable place to be. If you don't focus on the values at stake, you're likely to look for a way out. Often, this will mean moving in the direction of least resistance, just like water flowing over rock. That path may look easy, but it might not be the best thing for you.

Here's one reason why following the path of least resistance isn't necessarily the best idea: Once that path is in place and you follow it again and again, it gets deeper. This can create a well-worn groove that's hard to get out of.

Another reason is that taking the path of least resistance feeds into the natural tendency to pull back from pain. Conflict is stressful, and it's an obvious source of pain. Yet there's more going on here than the immediate pain of the conflict. Important values are at stake, and therefore your very life is at stake.

Pain that's occurring in the moment has a way of being a very loud voice that can drown out just about everything else. This can lead you to make choices that are more about getting relief than about living a valued life. Some choices may work against what you really care about, too.

Suppose you value keeping your commitments—your word manifesting in your actions. As you express this in your life, you notice a sense of satisfaction in knowing that people can count on you. You can be relied on and trusted. You follow through and do what you say you'll do.

And as you expand your reach, you notice that keeping commitments shows up across many areas of life. You keep commitments at work, with your partner, and with friends. You keep commitments in regard to what you eat, your exercise routine, and your recreational activities. And you even keep commitments during downtime, when you take some quiet moments just for you.

Now imagine that you find yourself in a situation where you might *fail* to keep a commitment you've made to someone else or even to yourself. You notice your body kicking into alarm mode. You feel an adrenaline rush, heightened energy, and focus. This reaction helps you work hard to keep that commitment, but suppose you can't—there's just no way. Not keeping your word seems inevitable.

What often happens next is that the mind gets caught up in finding a way out. You may think, "I could just not do what I said I would do." Or you might think, "Maybe I should just fess up and tell them I can't follow through." Or your mind might come up with other alternatives, like "I'll call in sick, make up a story, or find another excuse."

All of these thoughts are driven by discomfort linked with life circumstances that conflict with and threaten your values. If you look closely, some of the options on the table may violate not just the value at stake, but other values you also hold dear, like honesty or your sense of justice and fairness. Like a line of dominos set in motion by a single touch, our values can be knocked down one after another when we turn our lives over to pain, conflict, and mind chatter. This is where we can end up during values conflicts.

So the first lesson here is that values conflicts are inevitable. The second is that life can lead us in directions wildly divergent from the path we wish to take. The way out of this trap is to increase your awareness of values conflicts and how they play out in your own life. Below we cover three main types of conflicts to help you grow in awareness: conflicts between two or more values, conflicts between values and life roles or outside demands, and conflicts between values and what others wish you to do.

When Two or More Values Collide

Everyone experiences conflicts between two or more values. Life is rich, and because we tend to care about how we live in general, most of us hold core values in relation to many different domains: work, family, social relationships, personal growth, health, and more.

Work may keep you from your family, or time devoted to your values around family may keep you from nurturing friendships and forming new ones. Going back to school might keep you from exercise, time with or your kids. You may find that the time you devote to commitments to friends and loved ones eats away at the time you have for yourself and your own interests. In each case, two or more values compete for your time, energy, and resources.

Mark knew this type of conflict quite well. He found himself torn between wanting to be more involved with his two children and wanting to cultivate his creativity as a writer. He felt this conflict acutely in the evenings when he came home from work.

Or consider Susan, a wife, mother, and caregiver to her aging parents. She desperately wanted to do it all, but found herself falling short. Each commitment was important to her, and all three were demanding. This left her feeling like an octopus with six arms missing. Sound familiar?

Conflicts that include just two values can appear quite simple, but don't be lulled into thinking that. Seeing it as simple can quickly make you glib or dismissive. Values conflicts are not simple. Your life isn't simple, right? No matter how simple or straightforward a conflict between values appears to be, you need to spend some time exploring it. Don't dismiss it or jump for the easy or obvious solution. If you dig in a bit, you'll find that most values conflicts are rich, nuanced, and complex. They are hard and challenging for this reason.

Kirk, a forty-five-year-old electrician and an only parent, is a good example of what we're talking about here. He wanted to go back to school to get his bachelor's degree. He saw this move as a way to make himself eligible for a promotion at work, which would allow him to better provide for his three children. Kirk also loved reading and stretching his mind, and he looked forward to the humanities classes he'd have to take to fulfill his degree requirements.

But here's the rub: Kirk needed to keep working. To follow his dream, he'd have to attend evening classes. But to do that, he'd have to give up spending time with his kids in the evenings—a time that he cherished. He considered getting a babysitter or a nanny but cringed at the idea. It didn't feel right to him. He thought that parents ought to be there for their kids, and since he was the only parent in the house, that meant him.

So for Kirk, something that initially seemed an ideal way to live in alignment with his values created a values conflict that was quite a quagmire. His career and self-growth values were clashing with his values as a parent. In fact, his values as a parent showed up on both sides of the equation. And as if all of this weren't complicated enough, Kirk was also a diabetic. Because he valued his health and his ability to be healthy enough to parent his children, he was careful about his diet and maintaining his blood sugar levels. Being on a tight budget, Kirk struggled with managing his illness. Fresh produce was expensive, which made it difficult to eat right.

As you can see, there are many layers involved in Kirk's conflict. Protecting his health is necessary to support being there for his kids, but that requires money—and he'd also like to earn more to better provide for his kids. More education—something he also values—would fulfill many of these values, but at a cost to the time he spends with his kids. Many values conflicts are knotty like this.

When Values Clash with Roles and Outside Demands

We all have a role to play on the great stage we call life. In fact, it's highly likely that you have multiple roles and wear many hats. Think of the roles you play at work, at home, in relationships, in your community, and even in relation to yourself, and you'll see what we mean. But having multiple roles means that the demands of life are multiplied. We can't escape the fact that our values will collide with these roles and outside demands. It's not a matter of if, but when.

Conflicts between these roles and your values are difficult to navigate when the role is entwined with the necessities of life—such as making a living, taking care of your health, or being a parent or caregiver. In each case, the role takes time, energy, and resources and cannot be stepped out of easily.

All of this sets limits on what you can do and the time available to do it. In the meantime, life and the world around you keep marching on. It's like watching a slowly moving parade just outside your window. You see all of the wonderful possibilities, all of the happy people seemingly living their lives to the fullest. You feel as though you should be a part of it, but you're unable to join in the action. This can leave you feeling stuck, frazzled, and with a sense that life is just passing you by.

When you experience the pull of a value that conflicts with a role or obligation, you'll naturally feel conflict and stress. Anyone who's ever had a sick child home from school during the workweek knows what this is like.

The two most common conflicts we hear about center on not having enough time and on work demands. Obviously, those two can be related. Emily was intimately familiar with both. She and her husband were in serious debt, and although they were working feverishly to pay off their bills, they weren't getting ahead and decided they'd have to file for bankruptcy.

Then they caught a lucky break. Emily was offered a great promotion. Her salary would nearly double, but there was a price to pay. To get that salary boost, she'd have to relocate several hundred miles away, and she knew there was no way her family could relocate with her—at least not right away.

Her husband had to stay at his current job if they were ever to get out of debt, and she and her husband didn't want the kids to have to change schools and make new friends in the middle of the school year. All of this naturally consumed time. Working to get out of debt pulled Emily and her husband away from each other, and from their children too. When Emily made the difficult decision to relocate for her new job, she had drastically less time with the family.

We can also see this type of conflict with Tyrone, who, as he put it, "lived to rock climb." This was his passion, but like most of us he had to work to earn a living. He also had an aged mother who lived alone, and Tyrone wanted her to be able to live out her remaining years in her own home, as she wished to do. He felt a strong desire to be there for her and visited almost daily despite his busy work schedule as a computer programmer. He also supported her financially, and he saw his role as one of deep obligation and responsibility.

In the end, helping his mother retain a good quality of life and a sense of family connection was more important to Tyrone than using his time and money to go rock climbing. As he put it, "I still find time to keep in shape for rock climbing. The rocks will be around for a long time, but not my mother. She gave me everything growing up, and now it's my time to give back. Nothing else matters more to me right now."

These examples point to a common theme. We have commitments that place certain constraints on us, and we have other aspects of our lives we wish to nurture.

When People Want You to Go in Another Direction

Have you had a time when you wanted to go in one direction and other people wanted you to go in a different direction? These situations are commonplace, and often we negotiate them without major repercussions. For instance, you may want to go shopping with friends, but your friends want to go to the movies. Or perhaps you and your partner are planning to go out for dinner. You're thinking of this great little Italian restaurant, but your partner is really in the mood for Thai food. Most people navigate decisions in such situations fairly easily.

But in weightier situations, it can be hard to navigate conflicts between your values and what others would like you to do. Imagine that you greatly value spending time outdoors. With great anticipation, you look forward to the summer months when you can use your limited vacation time to camp, hike, fish, swim, or take your boat out for a spin on the water. You've made activities like this a part of your summers for most of your life. And now that you have a family, you've shared these experiences with your spouse and kids. They've even caught the outdoor bug too.

Until now. After several years of spending summers on the lake or in the mountains, your family wants to do something different. They want to go to Disney World. You cringe at the thought of spending your precious vacation time fighting the crowds and waiting in line for character meals or to go on rides promising mechanized thrills.

Don't get us wrong. Disney can be a fun place. The point here is that a conflict is brewing. These types of conflicts, where your values clash with the interests and demands of people you care about, can be especially hard. They want you to go with them in one direction, but you feel a strong pull in another direction. When that happens, you're likely to feel really torn apart.

Consider Angie, a thirty-four-year-old homemaker who's married to Rick, a fairly conservative engineer with a good job and income. They have two children, eight and six years old, and describe their marriage as loving and supportive. Angie left her job as an industrial designer without a second thought so she could be a stay-at-home mom with her "little angels," and she felt blessed that she had this option.

Once both kids were in school, Angie felt a vast emptiness in her days. She had lots of time on her hands and started thinking about what she'd like to do. Ultimately, Angie decided to go back to work as an industrial designer. It felt right.

But Rick wasn't crazy about the idea. He thought Angie should stay home, at least until the kids were in high school. Angie struggled with this too. The image of not being around to pick the kids up from school and not seeing them until she came home from work left her with a looming sense of guilt. When Rick voiced his opinion, it just intensified that guilt. This left her feeling stuck in her tracks.

How to Choose

The examples we've shared in this chapter show how difficult it can be to navigate values conflicts. They also reveal that almost anytime you feel deeply divided, you're facing a clash of values. Dig deeply enough, and you'll often find that life roles, outside demands, and the wishes of others also have a bearing on your values. You've taken on these life roles for a reason. If an outside demand weren't important to you, you'd probably find it easy to ignore or let go. The same can be said for the conflicts that arise when others want you to go in another direction.

Sometimes it simply seems that there's no good choice. Yet choose you must. Every day you have to make choices—some momentous, some seemingly more mundane. Even now, you're making a choice to read this book when you could be doing something else. The choice to read on doesn't mean the rest of your life is unimportant. In fact, it may mean that the rest of your life *is* important.

Metaphors for Navigating Values Conflicts

In the end, most of the choices we face daily are about time and energy. These are the factors that limit the extent to which we can pursue our various values. Time we spend on one can't be spent on another. It isn't possible to engage all of our values at once.

To help you clearly envision values conflicts, imagine that you have a large cube in front of you. Or if you're feeling ambitious, find a small cardboard box and do the exercise as we describe it.

This cube is your life, and its surface holds everything that matters to you. On each of the six sides, you paste one of your important self-growth or service-oriented values. If you want to include more than six, you can place them on the seams between sides.

Now imagine holding the cube right in front of your face, with one side clearly in view. Notice the value there. Also notice that you can't see the values on the other sides of the cube.

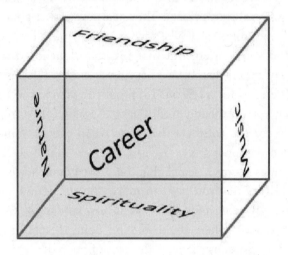

So, suppose you're looking at one side and it holds a career-related value. On the opposite side and out of view is a family-related value. The side to the left of career is being in tune with nature, and to the right is your love of music and creativity. Your spiritual value lies on the bottom, and on the top is your abiding interest in cultivating your long-term friendships.

While you're focused on career, it's next to impossible to see the other values. Yet they're still there and may be calling out to you for attention. You'll feel this call and the tension it creates. This is the seed for conflicts between values.

But notice that the cube isn't fixed in space and time. You can rotate it in your mind's eye and attend to any side you wish. You can even hold it in ways that allow you to see two or three sides at once. That's neat, because it suggests that some conflicts can be solved with a simple change in perspective.

To practice this in life, look for ways to combine several of your values, talents, and passions. The more you do that, the less conflicted you'll feel. Even seemingly mundane things might take on new meaning for you.

Still, sometimes we must choose between values. As the choosing process unfolds, our minds can play games with us—sometimes helpful, sometimes less so. Let's take a look at three metaphors that explore these games and ways of making choices when values are at stake: the relative importance game, the balancing act, and life as a dance.

The Relative Importance Game

In the relative importance game, choosing turns the options—in this case your values—into winners and losers. So when you choose one value over another, your mind is likely to follow with "Why didn't you choose that other value instead, isn't it important too? Do you really care about it? It doesn't seem like it!"

Your mind is actually helping you here, though it may not feel that way in the moment. It asks you to stop and consider whether a particular choice is as important as another. This is a good thing—much better than making choices on autopilot or based on whatever or whoever is screaming loudest at any given time. So play along. Stop and think about your choices and question yourself.

After thinking about it, you might answer your mind by saying, "Sure, mind, that other value is important. In fact, all of my values are important." Some of your values get short shrift in some situations, and some may be pushed aside repeatedly. Still, you can acknowledge that *all* of your values are important. The choice to go one way or another doesn't diminish any of your values. You simply have to prioritize. You can always come back to a value that seems to be getting the short end of the stick and spend time nurturing it. That's up to you.

The Balancing Act

Another game the mind will play is the balancing act. You've probably played this game many times. It has one simple rule: that you must keep your life in balance.

It's like a scale, and pans on each side get filled with the choices you make. When you choose the value on the left side more often, it will swing down, so you go back to the value on the right side and spend more time there to even things out. You're losing this game when your life appears to be out of balance. Most people who play this game feel as though they're constantly struggling. They have a sense of working hard to keep everything on an even keel and never quite doing it well enough or for long enough. It's exhausting and often painful.

So, what do you do here? First, look and see if you're playing this game and approaching your life like a balancing act. If so, is this a helpful metaphor for your life? Is it working? If not, then maybe it's time to stop playing this game. Maybe the swinging back and forth is your life—not balanced, but shifting, changing, and realigning with circumstances and your heart.

Life as a Dance

The third way to look at your choices is not as a game at all, but as an activity. We think of it as life as a dance. You flatten your values cube and lay it down with all of the sides up so that it turns into one big dance floor, with all of your values in clear view.

Just like in dancing, you step forward and back and side to side. You turn and sway to the rhythm of life. You go here, and then you move over there. Sometimes you might dance in one spot for quite a while; sometimes you use a lot of the floor but not one or two of the corners. You focus and redirect, engage and release, and throughout, you sink into the motion, the movement, and the experience.

Sometimes your pace is slow and deliberate, like a waltz. At other times it may seem frenetic, like a boogie or a foxtrot. Whatever the pace, you're moving between important areas of your life in a style that's distinctly your own. And you choose them like you accept an invitation to dance, sometimes with others, other times alone. Maybe life is like that—a dance.

The Importance of Flexibility

Regardless of the metaphor guiding your choices, life demands that you remain flexible. Just like an athlete preparing for a big event, you need to stretch and be limber or you risk hurting yourself—or in this case, your values. You play the game of life because there's really no other option, but how you play matters. If you go into it flexible, are wise in how you play, and are willing to leave it all on the field, the outcomes will take care of themselves.

The great enemy of flexibility is attachment. When we become too attached to outcomes, states of mind, or feelings, we lose sight of what we're doing and why we're doing it. We harden, become inflexible, and go into self-protection mode to preserve whatever we're attached to. This state of being tends to suck the life out of life.

This can even happen with values. Of course, a certain degree of attachment to our values is natural. After all, values are by definition important and dear to us. They embody who we are and who we want to be. We ought to protect them. They certainly deserve a voice. Just watch how far this goes and if it's helpful to you.

Values aren't dogma. If you allow them to become dogma or something you cling to, they'll lose their shine. Just think about it: You can't see a beacon or be guided by it if you're hanging on to it for dear life. You need perspective so that you can look for ways to express and manifest your values. You can't do that if values are like a clipboard pressed up to your nose. You won't be able to see anything beyond the board.

If you don't hold your values lightly and in a way that you can see them, you'll miss the fact that you can engage your values in many different ways, and in many different situations. Your values may start to feel oppressive. So think of holding your values lightly and with some flexibility, the way you might hold a tiny baby or a butterfly. Flit and dance among them. When you do, your life will always end up winning.

105

Choosing Between Several Values

You're naturally drawn to situations and events that reflect your values and are connected to your life purpose. Like a powerful magnet, they draw your interest and pull you in. By the same token, you naturally have less passion for experiences and activities that aren't aligned with your core values and purpose. You experience a magnetic repulsion, much like trying to join two magnets with like poles facing one another. No matter what you do, you'll never get them to stick.

So when faced with choices, listen to your heart. Then follow your inner voice and do what it says as much and for as long as possible. To do so, you'll need a clear awareness of what your core values are. The previous chapters were all about helping you develop this awareness. Still, in the heat of the moment, it can be easy to lose sight of what's important to you. There are a few helpful approaches at these times: visualizing what's important, prioritizing what matters, and combining valued domains.

Visualizing What's Important

When you feel pulled in different directions and don't know where to go, make a conscious choice to get in touch with your values. Slow things down. "Stop! Look! And listen to your heart!"

When you sense a values conflict, consciously remind yourself of your core values. Recall the inscription on your tombstone and reconnect with those words. Also bring to mind the valued intentions you've written down for the areas of life that are in conflict. Sense the difficulty in the choice you're about to make. Stop briefly, close your eyes, and sink into it as you might a comfortable chair after a long day.

As you do that, visualize different scenarios based on the different choices you could make in the situation. How would you feel if you chose one direction, and how would you feel if you chose another? What ripples would you create, and how far would they reach? Look for a sense of vitality and purpose, not just feeling good, as you do this.

If you allow yourself moments such as these to pause and connect, the choice that's right for you will manifest in your mind's eye, and in your gut. The conflict itself may not be entirely resolved, but you'll be clear about what's important to you. This clarity will usually point you in the right direction.

Prioritizing What Matters

You've probably heard people say things like "There aren't enough hours in the day." What this really means is that we're trying to do more than time will allow. Like a hummingbird, we dart from one activity to the next, often frenetically, yet there's never enough time to get to everything. The answer? We need to learn how to prioritize, and perhaps there's no more important place to do so than with your values.

Let's say you're in a situation where two valued intentions conflict. Close your eyes and bring the situation to mind, then imagine placing one intention on one end of a seesaw and the other on the other end. Just like children playing on a seesaw, both values probably move up and down, at least at first. Eventually though, things start to settle and one value starts to sink to the ground because it carries more weight. It resonates more fully with your core. This is the more important one. Which one is it for you?

Don't overthink this. Just follow your gut. Listen closely to what your inner voice is telling you and don't argue with it. That inner voice may be clear; you may not need a mental contest on a seesaw to know which is important in a specific situation. Or it could be that both are about equally important. Any outcome is fine. The key here is to think about what really matters to you.

Clear awareness of what matters is also important for helping you prioritize your values when time, energy, or resources are limited. In this context, prioritizing isn't so much a matter of saying which is most important (remember, they can all be important!); rather, think about which value seems to need the most attention at a given time, depending on the circumstances and your life situation.

Let's go back to Henry and see how this played out in his life. On one end of the seesaw, he placed his love of music and playing guitar. At the other end, he put his health. Up and down the ends went. He felt the pull of playing various guitars from his beloved collection and wanting to make this a bigger part of his life. And then he would swing back to his concern about being healthy and staying fit. Back and forth this went until eventually things settled. Health and fitness won out, and underneath that was a concern about his heart.

Why? His dad had his first heart attack when he was forty-eight, and Henry didn't want to go down the same path. He loved the energy and strength that came from having a healthy heart. So on days when his free time was limited, he chose to go for a run or a swim instead of playing guitar. This was his choice. He wasn't following anyone's instructions or doing what he "should" be doing. More than anything else, he wanted to stay healthy so he could enjoy his life (and music) for as long as he possibly could.

As you can see from Henry's example, prioritizing may involve seesawing between values, but eventually you touch down. It may entail making hard choices. Sometimes circumstances will dictate what's possible, and other times you'll have to make choices that accommodate other values, yours and those of others.

So many choices in life seem to be about winners and losers, but that isn't the case when prioritizing values. When you choose among two or more values, it's always a win-win situation. When the choice is between a value and something meaningless, you stand to lose. And though it may sound obvious, it's important to be clear on a third scenario: When you choose between two or more meaningless activities, you'll always lose.

This is why getting your values on your radar and keeping them there every day can make a huge difference in your life. When you put more of your values into your life, you win, regardless of what you choose.

If it's difficult or painful to think of setting aside a valued direction in a particular circumstance, you'll probably find it helpful to think in terms of the big picture. You may decide to dance with one value for a while. In time, you can decide to turn your attention to another value that's waiting for its turn. This is exactly what Angie did.

Developing her career as an industrial designer was one of Angie's core values up until the time her first child was born. Angie then danced with her value of being the kind of mom who would stay home with her kids, and as she did, that value grew in strength and importance. Although she chose to put her career on hold until her kids were in elementary school, that was a choice that resonated with her core. A waltz and a samba later, she was back into her career and moving into a new chapter of life as a parent with growing kids.

Combining Valued Domains

The human mind loves to categorize and compartmentalize, and it can do that with just about anything, including our values. This can lead us into thinking that what we value in parenting is somehow separate from what we value about career, and what we value in career is separate from what we value in friendships, or health, or recreation, and on down the line. This is an illusion and a trap. It does nothing but add to the sense of paralysis and lopsidedness we experience whenever different values collide.

But remember, your core values, as well as your talents, passions, and purpose, are like golden threads that run through your life and daily activities. They're interwoven, and this is a large part of what gives your life its strength, and its beauty. If you look closely, you'll see that your values in many different areas of life resound with one theme, and that many of your talents and passions manifest within a single value. This opens the door to creative and liberating solutions to perceived conflicts between values.

Joe, a medical supplies salesman, arrived at this solution almost by accident. His daughter, Hannah, wasn't bashful about letting him know that he didn't spend enough time with her. And for every time she complained, it replayed dozens or hundreds of times in his mind. It distracted him—and it pulled at him.

Sometimes Joe gave in and did typical things with Hannah, like playing board games. Yet all the while he'd be thinking of how empty this activity was and how he'd rather be doing something else, even if it was just being alone to clear his head and unwind after a long day of talking, meeting people, and hustling around on sales calls.

Then, late one Sunday afternoon when Joe was settling down to read the newspaper, he caught a glimpse of Hannah in the other room, sitting down at the piano and tapping a few keys. That piano was passed down from his parents and had more or less become a dust collector in their home. Until that moment, it had never occurred to Joe that Hannah might be interested in learning to play. So he put down the paper, sat down next to her, and asked her if she'd like to learn to play. Her eyes lit up.

Joe helped Hannah find a piano teacher, and once she started taking lessons he often arrived early to pick her up so that he could listen to her playing. And when he got home from work, he often heard Hannah practicing away. This brought back memories of his childhood and how his mother played piano. He realized he loved the feel of a house filled with music. Inspired by Hannah's dedication, he decided to dust off his old guitar and start practicing instead of withdrawing with the daily paper.

After a while, they started to play together. Joe was surprised at how playing music with his daughter made him feel more alive and energized after work. She was happy, and so was he. In those shared musical moments, Joe found a way to connect with his daughter, and with his old love for music. He also discovered that this helped him wind down in the evenings in a more satisfying way than just spending time alone.

Luis, on the other hand, put a lot of thought into how he could create just this sort of solution. When his wife got pregnant, he knew he needed to change careers so he could support his family. In the past he'd worked part-time as a horse trainer so he could devote his time to volunteering at a local Boys and Girls Club.

As the coordinator of athletic activities at the club, Luis was beloved by the kids. He was the purveyor of new basketballs, athletic shoes, and tickets to local sporting events. He thrived on that. But even more, he valued being a role model, raising the kids' confidence and spirits, and helping them find direction and purpose in their lives. He saw the difference he was making, and that filled him with pride.

He found a lot of joy in this work and didn't want to give it up, but he knew he couldn't sustain it with a baby on the way. He had to find a full-time job with a decent salary. After many hours racking his brain, he decided on a compromise. He sought out training as a social worker and ended up working with kids much like those he mentored at the club. This allowed him to combine one of his values, helping kids in need, with his values around parenting and the external necessities of life—namely, making a living. He had to scale back significantly, but on weekends, he still helped out at the club.

The central message here is this: Look for ways to combine your values. Also, remember that some values can be expressed wherever you find yourself, no matter what the circumstances. Love, kindness, compassion, helpfulness, fidelity, commitment, honor, trust, a giving spirit, or a helping hand—all have a place even in the most difficult life situations. Even creativity, problem solving, loyalty, humor, playfulness, and spirituality can find their way into many roles and activities. When you combine your values in this way, you may find you face fewer dilemmas. You just have to look for the opportunities.

See your life as a garden: Cultivate the soil, then plant the seeds that lie at the heart of your values. Water them. Tend them. And if you do that, you'll see them grow.

Dangerous Choices

Life is all about choices. You make them every day. Some decisions are good for you, others not so good. When you choose to live out your values, it will be good for you, no matter what the outcome. It won't always be easy, but it will be vital, rich, meaningful, connected, whole, and dignified.

But there are two types of choices that aren't so good: procrastinating and making foul compromises. We call them dangerous choices because they work against you in the long run. Procrastinating involves postponing or deferring the pursuit of what matters to you. Making foul compromises means that instead of following your heart, you do what's easy or feels good. Both should be avoided.

Procrastinating

Procrastinating is probably the worst and most fateful choice people make. They endlessly defer doing what's important to them. How many times have you heard someone say, "I'll do that after I graduate from college or after I get a job." And then after they've graduated and gotten that job, they say, "I'll do that after I get my promotion." One promotion, two promotions, three promotions later, they say, "I'll definitely do that after I retire." You can see where this is heading, can't you?

Many people push their dreams off to the side and into the future. Too often, time runs out and we die without pursuing our dreams. What does the inscription on your tombstone say if this happens? It doesn't say what you really wanted it to say. How could it?

Take a moment to reflect on this. Ask yourself, "Am I doing this too? Am I putting off living out my values until after...[fill in the blank]?" Be honest as you take stock. If you find that you're stuck in the procrastination trap, don't beat yourself up; you're certainly not alone.

Most of us delay doing this or that—including important things—once in a while. But for some of us this can become a habit. Often it's fueled by fears: fear of failure, fear of inadequacy, fear of taking a chance or a bold step, fear of revealing vulnerability, fear of being rejected, fear of being criticized, the list goes on and on.

Procrastination can also be used as a defense—a way to stave off the demands and pressures coming from other people. Some people actually procrastinate because they love the adrenaline rush of having to deal with piles of unfinished business in one frenetic push. And people may defer doing what matters because, well, they don't really know what matters to them. That may have been your situation when you decided to read this book. Regardless of where procrastination comes from, it's never helpful if the result is that your values get put on hold.

As you continue reading this book, we'll help you get to the core of why you procrastinate and provide some strategies for getting unstuck. For now, you just need to make a choice and decide if enough is enough. Being young is no protection from the costs of this dangerous choice. Young or old, none of us really know how much time we have left on this planet.

Sure, thinking about your own mortality can seem gloomy and morose. But it also opens the door to incredible richness and depth. Knowing that you will die—and that you know not when—and reminding yourself of that each day, makes it possible for you to focus on how you will live. Not tomorrow, but how you'll live right now, starting today, in this very moment. What do you want to do with the time that you do have?

This awareness of your own mortality can be your best teacher. It's like a daily kick in the butt. Do you delay doing what you value for another day, or do you use your time as best as you can? If you opt for the latter, you'll add vitality to your life. As that old saying goes, you can't necessarily add years to your life, but you can add life to your years. That's what's really at stake here. The time to live out your values is now, today—not tomorrow, next month, next year, or twenty years from now. You don't have to join the ranks of the millions of people who have died without having lived out their dreams. This is a choice you can make.

Making Foul Compromises

Most solutions to values conflicts require making compromises. There's nothing wrong with compromise, provided that it's fair and balanced, and that the choice embodies one or more of your values in some way. But foul compromises are different, and they're never good for you.

Foul compromises are choices based on convenience. We choose the easy way out. We choose the path of least resistance. We make choices because they seem to promise relief from pain or conflict. Or we decide to avoid conflict altogether. This is a slippery slope.

We aren't asking you to be a martyr or a masochist. It's natural to try to minimize pain and conflict. We're wired to do that to some degree. But sometimes avoiding pain and conflict entails costs that are too high.

One potentially harmful choice is a turn down "feel-good street." Conflict and pain love to point us down this street. If you allow conflict to steer you down that street, you'll find some relief, a brief vacation from the stressful discomfort of the values conflict. But you won't find your values on feel-good street.

Let's take another look at Angie, who wants to go back to developing her career. This intention is in conflict with other values Angie holds related to family. Suppose Angie agrees to her husband's request to stay at home for no reason other than to avoid marital conflict and her own guilt. If she did that, she'd be choosing the path of least resistance and making a foul compromise.

When we choose the path of least resistance, eventually we end up feeling like we're off course. We lose track of our values and may even compromise them, and all of this adds to a sense of dissatisfaction with life. The more often you choose this path, the more dissatisfied you'll feel.

Plus, the relief you get will be only temporary. With Angie, it's easy to imagine her remaining a stay-at-home mom. And it's easy to imagine her feeling better at first, but eventually feeling worse. Like a tumor that goes undetected, her dissatisfaction could grow until it displaces many of her good feelings. Over time, it could sow the seeds of resentment toward her husband, and maybe even her children. She'd also be likely to feel deeply disappointed in herself. This is where foul compromises get you. You feel good at first, but eventually you feel bad about not doing what matters. This wouldn't be good for Angie, and it won't be good for you either.

Consider Luis, soon to be a father and facing a conflict between making a living to support his family and his volunteer work with children. He ended up making a fair compromise that supported his values, but it could have gone the other way. Instead of deciding to become a social worker, he could have opted to work full-time in another line of work, perhaps where he didn't have to complete a professional training course first. If he had done that, he would have risked being bogged down in a career he hated in order to support his family. Luis avoided that kind of foul compromise, and you can too.

You Have a Voice When Navigating Values Conflicts

In the vacuum of space, there is a region of our solar system known as the asteroid belt. Scattered about this vast and expansive region are chunks of rocks of various sizes and shapes. They move in predictable orbits, and sometimes they collide with one other. These collisions reverberate and alter the trajectory of other asteroids. Some of these find their way to earth—sometimes with catastrophic results.

Space has been called a violent place for this reason, and our lives can seem that way too, especially when core values collide. But living a valued life isn't about avoiding values conflicts. It's about how you navigate these conflicts.

Values can and will collide with each other, and when they do, each will call out for your attention and resources. Many of these collisions just happen; others are created by other choices you've made. Knowing what matters in the context of a specific conflict and circumstances can help you choose wisely, act purposefully, and keep moving forward.

There's no escaping the fact that living your values is hard work. Values conflicts can be painful and uncomfortable. Yet they can also be one of your greatest teachers. Without them, you'd likely never know what really, truly matters to you. Life would feel like a series of random collisions, without meaning or purpose.

So be clear about your values. Recognize conflicts when they occur. Seek to resolve them with as much creativity and flexibility as you can muster. And never forget this: Any conflict between two or more values is a win-win situation. Where you stand to lose big-time is when you choose activities that don't have meaning for you over those that do—and especially if you do this over and over again.

Chapter 7

What Are the Barriers to Living Your Values?

There are no constraints on the human mind, no walls around the human spirit, no barriers to our progress except those we ourselves erect.

—Ronald Reagan

You cannot be wimpy out there on the dream-seeking trail. Dare to break through barriers, to find your own path.

—Les Brown

I have learned that life may not always be easy, but it's always worth living.

—Melanie Race

If living a values-based life were easy, if the obstacles were few or minor, we'd all be doing it. But that's not how it works. Living in alignment with your values often requires effort and a willingness to face pain. In fact, nearly every value worth pursuing has some fear attached to it, some cost that makes it a hard place to go. If you let these barriers defeat you, you won't live your life. That's why it's important to understand them and learn how to work your way around them—or even work with them.

We'll start by helping you identify specific barriers to acting on your values. What's getting in *your* way as you begin to move down a valued path? What shows up to make you hesitate as you plan or imagine the first steps toward something that matters?

The Importance of Seeing Your Barriers

Barriers can exert an enormous influence on your life. That's why it's critical to recognize and find words for them. Sometimes they affect you in insidious, even unconscious ways. You may choose to avoid opportunities to engage your values without knowing exactly why. You just don't feel like it. But, over time, this catches up with you.

Or you may find a possibility for valued living interesting, but for some reason you put it off until the opportunity slips away. Sometimes there's a vague discomfort you can't really express. Many of these choices are influenced by hidden fears, aversions, and other kinds of pain that you simply aren't aware of.

Sally, a fifty-year-old flight attendant, was blocked by a fear tucked away in the recesses of her past. She valued her spiritual life a great deal and expressed those values whenever and wherever she could. But, oddly, when her pastor offered her a chance to teach Sunday school, she declined flat out.

Sally explained that her work schedule was erratic, and that often she'd be called upon at the last minute to fly on Sundays. Her pastor offered a solution. He could have a retired Sunday school teacher waiting in the wings as backup for times when Sally couldn't make it. After an awkward pause, Sally followed with another excuse, this time focusing on needing time with her children on Sundays.

Sally's reasons seem reasonable enough, but in reality they were just smoke and mirrors. Hidden beneath them was a larger and more menacing barrier—one she hardly thought of, even as it influenced her decisions. Sally was born with a congenitally deformed foot and bore the brunt of endless teasing because of it. This problem was later corrected, but not the lingering emotional damage left in its wake. Her whole life had been marked by a fear of ridicule, especially from children. The offer to teach Sunday school reawakened those buried fears and painful emotional scars.

Other blocks to valued living may be painfully obvious. Depression, emptiness, shame, and the fear of failure can cast a long shadow across your path.

Certain patterns of thought can be even more inhibiting. What-if thoughts that detail catastrophic possibilities can stop us in our tracks: "What if I'm not good enough?" "What if I can't do it?" "What if I don't know how?" "What if I look like a fool?" "What if I disappoint others?" Thoughts like these ring inside all of us, over and over again. They grab our attention and sap our vitality and motivation. And they can be relentless, too. Like waves crashing on the ocean shore, they keep coming and coming, beating us down until we're paralyzed with certainty that nothing will ever change.

If we don't face these demons, we end up doing nothing. Each opportunity to pursue what matters slips away, making living a valued life ever more elusive. The rest of this chapter is devoted to helping you identify the barriers that seem to stand in the way of your desire to travel in a valued direction.

Revealing Your Barriers

Before you can learn about your barriers, you have to be clear about a direction you want to take. Start by thinking about one of the values you uncovered in chapters 3 and 4. Now identify a situation or relationship where you might wish to act on that value but hesitate because it feels challenging.

Sink into that one value. Touch the sweetness of it unencumbered by any obstacles or challenges you might face. Imagine the "ideal you" enacting your value freely, fully, and without defense. What would you do or say with that person or in that setting if you were acting on your value?

Go slowly and deliberately, and get specific. What's the first thing the "ideal you" would do? If someone else is involved, notice what that person says or does and what do you say or do back. As you continue to go into the situation, notice what gets in the way as the "ideal" you slips back into the "normal" you.

Begin by looking at the emotions that arise as you try to act on your values in the situation you're visualizing. Is there fear, shame, sadness, or anger? Do you feel vulnerable to hurt or disapproval? Try to label the emotions you feel. Also look for a sense of hardening, tightness, or pulling back. These are your emotional barriers. Fear of these emotional responses probably has something to do with why you haven't taken more effective action in the pursuit of this value.

Now observe what you're thinking as the situation unfolds. Are there thoughts about negative outcomes or worries about how others might react? Are there memories of past failures or times when you didn't persevere or follow through? Are there self-judgments? Are you evaluating others? These are your cognitive barriers. Fear of these thoughts, judgments, and potential outcomes may be standing in the way of enacting your values.

Now look for any behavioral obstacles. As you visualize acting on your value, are there things you don't know how to do, things you need to learn? For example, do you need greater skill at communicating your feelings and desires? Or do you need to learn how to cope with distressing feelings? Are there prerequisites, things that have to happen first before you can act on your values? Are there resources you need? These are your behavioral barriers.

So far so good. Now write down the main barriers you've discovered—emotional, cognitive, and behavioral. Next, go ahead and visualize one or two additional situations where you'd like to act on this same value. As you do each visualization, explore the emotional, cognitive, and behavioral blocks that show up. If you discover any new barriers, add them to your list.

It may seem daunting to bring your barriers to the light of day and list them in this way. You may worry or feel overwhelmed. That's okay, and an important sign that you're on the right track. Barriers are usually things that we'd rather not think about. So when you think about them, you'll feel and think in ways that may not leave you uplifted and energized. This is important work and a signal that you're doing something important for yourself.

Keep in mind that you don't have to fix or overcome these blocks right now. The next three chapters will give you tools to do that. For now, just being aware of your barriers is all that matters. You can't surmount what you don't see, and you can't change what you don't understand.

Bernadette's Journey into Her Barriers

Let's have a look at how this exercise went for Bernadette, a forty-two-year-old waitress. Five years ago she was happily married to the man of her dreams. A phone call later he was gone. A drunk driver had killed her husband as he was riding his bicycle home from work. Married one moment and widowed the next. Being robbed of her soul mate was a bitter pill.

Bernadette did the best she could in the wake of that tragedy and now lives with a man she met in a grief group. The values she wants to bring into her relationships are compassion and understanding of another person's point of view. But both values tend to fly off her radar quickly, especially during conflict. Bernadette tends to get angry and blame her boyfriend for not seeing her needs. The anger hurts him and triggers withdrawal. This is the pattern she wants to change.

To get started, she visualized a previous conflict and imagined new, values-based responses on her part. In the opening moments of the clash, Bernadette sees herself asking about her boyfriend's needs and point of view. What does he think is going on, and what is he hoping for in the situation?

As he begins to answer, she observes the emotions that come up for her. The first is helplessness, a sense that nothing will ever change, that the pain of loneliness she struggles with will just go on. Right next to this is sadness, a feeling that she will never be seen and understood the way she was by her husband. And then following right behind, like a fast-moving train is anger—that this man, with whom she shares her life and bed, simply doesn't get her.

She feels the raucous energy of anger welling up inside her. And as it begins to reach a crescendo, she notices a desperate urge to shout at him, to try to crack through. With this comes the thought that she's broken by her grief, that she can never recover, and the thought that she's wasting her time and love on this man.

After Bernadette settled herself a bit, one behavioral block became clear. She didn't know how to communicate in a way that upheld her values. She just didn't know how to express her needs without anger. She sensed that there must be a way, but she had no idea what that might be.

After viewing the scene and her reactions, Bernadette had a far clearer sense of what blocked her compassion and desire to understand her boyfriend's point of view. She had emotional walls built around helplessness, sadness, and anger. If Bernadette were to act on her values of compassion and empathy, she'd have to encounter all three of these painful feelings. And when they showed up, she'd have to face the urge to shout and blame.

But that's not all. She'd have to face her cognitive barriers and behavioral blocks, too. She'd have to face the walls fabricated from thoughts like "I'm broken beyond recovering" and "I'm just wasting my time." Each of these thoughts had a sting of its own, and together they formed a toxic cocktail of deep despair. Her behavioral barrier was simply this: She didn't know how to express vulnerability. She always did it in a fashion that drove her boyfriend away.

No wonder Bernadette had difficulty acting on her values. Each step forward invited pain, opening up a deep, old wound that never seemed to heal completely. That kept her stuck, with a sense that her life was nothing more than a rehashing of old hurts. If she wanted to live her values, she'd have to face her painful thoughts and emotions, and she'd need to learn a whole new way to communicate. In short, she'd have to do something new with her barriers to get something new in her life.

Matters became a bit more challenging when she used the visualization exercise to explore conflicts in two other relationships—with her younger sister and with her boss at the restaurant.

With her sister, Bernadette discovered the feeling of resentment as a barrier. When her husband was killed, her sister wasn't there for her. The fact that they were ten years apart in age was no salve for the wound created by her sister's lack of support during that difficult time. Since then, every conflict with her sister triggered an unforgiving feeling that loomed large and tended to block empathy and connection.

With Bernadette's boss, a different barrier presented itself. The man was a nervous wreck, always obsessing about minor problems at the café. His most unfortunate quality was an accusing style. Each harsh word and pointed finger was like a barbed porcupine quill, piercing Bernadette and being drawn in deeper and deeper. This left her feeling wounded, incompetent, and wrong.

So now there were two more emotional blocks to face if Bernadette was going to bring compassion and understanding to her relationships: resentment and vulnerability to criticism. It was a tall order, yet it also gave Bernadette self-compassion. She could see why there had been such a gap between her behavior and the values she cared about. It also gave her hope. Now that she understood what her barriers were, she had a much better chance of overcoming them.

Self-Awareness Is the First Step

Doing this exercise isn't a bed of roses. If you do it honestly, it will be difficult. But that's not all. If you look at it a little deeper, it is vital, too. If you've ever worked really hard at something, you know what we're talking about. You're tired, yes. But it's a good tired. It's not just bitter; it's bittersweet.

That's what doing this exercise offers you. You'll be armed with knowledge and a clearer sense of what stands between you and living out your values, your dreams, your purpose, your life. This is an important first step in doing what matters.

Knowledge alone won't be enough. Facing your barriers will require commitment, a sense that you've had enough of the same old, same old and are ready for change. In chapters 8 through 10, we'll help you develop this by giving you a set of skills for noticing and acknowledging the feelings, thoughts, and behavioral obstacles that get in your way. Acceptance will also be important; by that we mean the willingness to take these painful thoughts and feelings *with you* as you move toward what matters.

Who's Driving Your Life Bus? A Metaphor for Change

To help you understand the role of acceptance, take a moment and imagine that you're driving a bus. We'll call it your life bus. (This metaphor and exercise are inspired by Steven Hayes, Kirk Strosahl, and Kelly Wilson, in their book *Acceptance and Commitment Therapy*.) The bus is a metaphor for your life, and you're at the wheel, choosing its direction. As you drive along, see yourself trying to steer the bus toward a value, something you want to do, learn, or become.

Allowing the Monsters to Take Control of Your Life Bus

Here's the challenge: As you head in the direction of your values, some big, ugly monsters show up in front of you. These are the barriers we've been talking about. There's a fear monster looming out there, and maybe one that feels like hopelessness or despair. Maybe there's a disappointment or loss monster, or one that feels like exhaustion. You might even find a monster who screams, "You can't do it," or keeps shouting about bad things that will happen, or perhaps a monster screams hateful judgments at you.

So there they are, gnashing their terrible teeth and roaring their terrible roars. Menacing, loathsome, and horrible, they stalk you at every turn. Not only are they blocking your way and paralyzing your progress, now they're even pushing you off course. You're filled with a desire to escape, to be anywhere but here and having to face them. To escape, to ease the pain and discomfort, all you have to do is turn the bus—your life—in another direction.

But painful experiences occur with some frequency in our lives, and all that turning away is costly. When we choose to turn away from them, we engage in what's known as experiential avoidance. We decide to get away from the monsters, go somewhere else.

Being the creative creatures that we are, we can find many ways to cut and run to avoid the pain. You're probably familiar with some of them, either directly or indirectly: shutting down, numbing out with drugs or alcohol or TV, picking a fight, running away, overeating, overworking, "retail therapy," lying on the couch, compulsive pleasure seeking or thrill seeking—the list goes on and on.

Regardless of how we do it, there's no escaping the fact that when we engage in avoidance, we're turning our lives over to the monsters. They, not us, are running the show. And even if they seem to disappear from time to time, they never go away entirely. They're always lurking in the dark corners of your past and watching for another opportunity to obstruct or divert your life bus in the present.

But it doesn't stop there. Each time you relinquish your life to the monsters, you feed experiential avoidance one more time. With time and practice, avoidance grows a belly and becomes a damaging, self-defeating habit of turning away when life is calling you to lean in.

This habit of turning away from pain brings new costs. You may not have the monsters to contend with, but you pay in the coin of loss: lost meaning, lost self-respect, damaged relationships, and alienation from the things you care about. Not living your life hurts.

Plus, most avoidance strategies have their own specific costs. Some of these effects are obvious, like the impact of alcohol or drug abuse. Some are more subtle but can still be profound, such as shutting down your moods, the effect of workaholism on your partner, or surrounding yourself with the familiar and comfortable.

Taming Your Wild Things

Maurice Sendak's classic children's book *Where the Wild Things Are* offers a lesson about the costs of running from our pain. Max, the main character, is like any normal ten-year-old. When life didn't go his way, he escaped from reality by visiting an imaginary world. In that world, he was confronted by aspects of his pain and sadness in various hideous forms—the Wild Things!

Eventually Max learned to tame his Wild Things by not running from them—in other words, by no longer succumbing to experiential avoidance. He returns from his fantasy world back to his bedroom, where he finds his supper waiting, still hot. You can learn to tame your monsters too.

Suppose, like Max, you decide to move in a valued direction in spite of the monsters. How do you deal with them when they're shouting and carrying on and blocking your way? There's only one solution: Let the monsters on the bus so they can't block you anymore.

Just open the door and accept them as part of your life. Eventually they'll take their seats in the back. They'll still jump up and wave their arms from time to time. They'll yell their threats and epithets and try to scare and discourage you. You can see them in the mirror, and you can hear their cacophony. And sometimes they'll probably try to tell you where or how to drive the bus. They may even try to grab the wheel.

But here's what has changed: The monsters aren't in front of you anymore, keeping you stuck. You can put the bus in gear and head straight for what you value. You're taking them with you, along with all of their upset, *and* you can still move. You're the driver, and ultimately you are the one in charge of where the bus will go.

This is the choice you and everyone else must always face: Accept the pain, take it with you, and go where your values send you. Or turn away from the pain and from what matters. To live a valued life, you have to say yes to the monsters and take them aboard. You have to say yes to their attacks, yes to fear, and yes to the emotions you don't want to feel.

This is what we mean by acceptance—saying yes. It's how you turn intentions into actions, how you get from avoidance to what matters.

Willingness with the Monsters

To help you get a better sense of the role of values and avoidance in your life, we're going to ask you to go a little further with the monsters on the bus metaphor. Start by choosing a value that you want to strengthen and that you've tended to avoid acting on. Write this value in the space provided in the following diagram. Now recall situations where you could have turned this value into action, or imagine situations where you could do this. Keep exploring these possibilities until you become aware of some of your emotional and mental blocks—your monsters. Give each monster a name, and write those names in the boxes in the diagram below.

Here's the most important part. In the area under "experiential avoidance strategies," list some of the ways you've tried to steer away from the monsters. What do you do when painful thoughts and emotions come up? What are your specific methods of avoidance? Finally, under "costs," write down the losses and specific negative outcomes you've experienced after using your experiential avoidance strategies.

YOUR VALUE

MONSTERS

1. _____

2. _____

3. _____

4. _____

5. _____

6. _____

EXPERIENTIAL AVOIDANCE STRATEGIES

1. _____
2. _____
3. _____
4. _____
5. _____
6. _____

COSTS

1. _____
2. _____
3. _____
4. _____
5. _____
6. _____

So far, so good. Now go back to your diagram and take another look at the monsters you've been avoiding. After reviewing all of them, one by one, ask yourself whether you'd be willing to bring these painful experiences with you on the bus—your life—in order to live your value. To put it another way, if you could turn your valued intention into action by taking the monsters with you, letting them snipe at you as you go, would you be willing? Is there anything about the monsters that you absolutely cannot have along for the ride?

How did you answer? Be honest. If your authentic answer is yes, meaning that you're willing to take your monsters with you on the bus, you've taken a huge step toward changing your life. If the answer is no or maybe, don't worry. Help is on the way. The next three chapters will give you a chance to develop a new relationship with your monsters, one that could make you a lot more willing to bring them along on your life's path.

Stanley Unpacks the Costs of Unwillingness

Before we wrap up this chapter, let's see how Stanley, a forty-something bookstore owner, used the monsters diagram to explore willingness. His value was to somehow help to protect the earth. A logging company near his town was in a court battle with environmentalists over a plan to clear-cut part of an old-growth forest. Stanley wanted to join the environmental group. Like the main character in Dr. Seuss's *The Lorax*, he wanted to speak for the voiceless trees and the forest that he loved. Joining the protests at the courthouse seemed like a good way to do that, or so he thought.

As Stanley considered his plan, he noticed that his ideas, the strong voice and passion within him, were being drowned out by ominous thoughts and feelings. His monsters had shown up. Stanley was shy, and he feared being judged by some of the strong personalities in the anti-logging group.

And he was afraid. He feared that his livelihood and income would take a hit if he spoke out. Seared in his mind was the thought that mill workers might stay out of his store if he aligned himself with the "tree huggers." People might say rude things to him on the street. He thought, "I'm lonely enough as it is without the whole town turning against me. I'm never going to make a difference, anyway."

As Stanley carefully reviewed his thoughts and feelings, he noted the following experiential avoidance strategies:

1. Putting things off

2. Pretending to myself that I'll do something

3. Lying on the couch and watching TV

4. Making excuses

5. Eating too much

Then he assessed the costs of these avoidance strategies and came up with the following list:

1. Loneliness because I don't get involved

2. Feeling a lack of meaning

3. Feeling disgusted with my cowardice

4. Boredom

5. Weight gain

6. Feeling helpless

When it came to the question of willingness to invite the monsters on his bus, Stanley said no. With that, one thing became very clear: His experiential avoidance strategies were costing him dearly. He was paying with loneliness, self-hate, depression, and negative health effects. Though he wasn't ready to try acceptance with his monsters yet, he did start to wonder if the costs of *not* doing so might be far greater than the discomfort of facing them.

Facing the Monsters Matters

As you reach the end of this chapter, it might be valuable to consider the costs of your own experiential avoidance. Are you paying too much? Might facing the monsters be less painful than the price you pay when you run from them? Might you be willing to accept your monsters in order to stop paying that price?

There's no escaping this simple truth about life: As you step in the direction of something you care about, you risk feeling, thinking, or doing something you'd rather not think, feel, or do. When people say, "Life is hard," they're speaking to this basic truth. It's not that life itself is hard. The hard part is finding a way forward with the monsters that seem to get in the way.

Vitality quickly morphs into despair when we hand over our lives to the monsters and let them stand in the way of where we want to go or steer us in directions we'd rather not go. But it doesn't have to be that way.

There is a way forward if you're willing to risk thinking what you think and feeling what you feel as you do what you value. This is the secret to a vital life, and it can get you unglued from the insanity of expecting things will somehow change for the better as you keep doing more of the same. And you can put it into a single word: "willingness."

Chapter 8

Willingness with Cognitive Barriers

A barrier is of ideas, not of things.

—Mark Caine

If you change the way you look at things, the things you look at change.

—Wayne Dyer

Be master of mind rather than mastered by mind.

—Zen proverb

Among the most challenging barriers to living your values are the products of your own mind. Our minds try to predict the future, looking beyond the present moment to see what might happen. This isn't inherently a bad thing. Often, looking ahead to see dangers or problems can protect us from pain.

But here's the rub: Every time you make a plan to act on your values, you enter a state of uncertainty. You're not sure what will happen, and your mind starts its fortune-telling process, trying to figure out what bad things could occur. If you listen, you might hear things like these: "You'll fail." "People might get angry." "You'll lose money." "You'll be lonely." "You'll be bored." This blabber can take many forms. Your mind can come up with more scary possibilities than a shyster insurance salesman.

Your mind also makes judgments. This can happen even as you imagine taking steps toward something you care about. Because it hasn't happened yet, your mind naturally tries to figure out if the plan is good or bad. Again, this can be helpful, but it can also work against you.

Let's say you decide to advocate for a recycling center for your community. Your mind is compelled to evaluate: "That's stupid. Here you go, tilting at windmills again with another grandiose, hare-brained plan." Or say you decide to insist on an earlier bedtime for your child. Your mind may follow with thoughts like "That's mean. You're being a bad parent. You just want him out of your hair so you can have more time to yourself. How selfish of you."

So that's how it works: For virtually any plan that carries you in a direction that matters, your mind is likely to scare you with some future nightmare, or to judge you and insinuate that you're doing the wrong thing. Although prediction and evaluation have a role in protecting you from danger, the mind tends to have trouble making a distinction between situations that are truly potentially dangerous and those that are mere mental concoctions. This can create needless internal conflicts that have a way of stopping you in your tracks.

By its very nature, the human mind is unruly and doesn't bend easily to efforts at control. It just keeps chattering with endless strings of warnings and pejoratives. And we really don't have much choice about what we think. Many thoughts just pop into and out of our awareness. Some are pleasant, and others quite unwelcome.

Even now, as you read, "Twinkle, twinkle, little...," you can learn something about how the mind works. You didn't choose to think "star," but it showed up in an instant, manufactured as a product of your history and your mind just doing what minds do. Now imagine if "star" were a difficult thought for you, a shameful recollection, or a painful truth, and you can see where this simple process might take you. This gives you some insight into why we say you typically don't have any choice when it comes to thoughts.

If this leaves you feeling a bit hopeless, don't let it. Your mind can be your worst enemy or your greatest friend. The final arbiter here is not *what* you think, but your *relationship* with what you think. This point is hugely important for you to understand.

You have only limited choice about what you think, but you have limitless control over the kind of relationship you have with your inner narrative, the ongoing monologue of your mind. You can choose how you respond to your thoughts. When the thought monsters are standing in front of your bus blocking the way to valued goals, there's no getting rid of them. The only thing you can do is watch your mind with disinterest and compassion and see if its message is helpful to you or not.

Nurturing a New Relationship with Your Mind

Whenever your mind blocks valued action, regardless of whether it uses judgments or fear and fortune-telling, your first response should be to observe your thoughts. Once you can observe them, you can begin to develop some perspective on them, and a new relationship with them. There are a number of techniques that can help you do that. We'll outline a few that we like: the white room meditation, thought labeling, repetition, understanding the purpose of the thoughts and thanking your mind for them, carrying thoughts with you, and exploring the workability of your thoughts.

White Room Meditation

Imagine you're in a medium-size white room with no furniture or decorations, just bare walls. There's a door to your left and another to the right; both open to darkness beyond.

Now imagine your thoughts entering that room as they arise. They come in from the darkness at your left and depart into the darkness to your right. Give each thought an image. It could be a bird or a cloud or a little black terrier. It doesn't matter. Just let each thought be some simple object that enters, crosses your field of vision, and then exits. If you get tired of one object, switch to another.

As you watch each thought, neither resist it nor get involved with it. Just let it make its way across the room until it disappears into the darkness at your right. Be a witness to your thoughts, without judging, retreating from them, or engaging them. Watch until the individual thoughts begin to lose their importance and you experience a growing detachment from them. Here in the white room, you can know your thoughts for what they are: creatures of the mind who have their brief moment and disappear.

Do the white room meditation for four to five minutes, or as long as it takes to get comfortable with it. As you do, notice that you can observe your thoughts just as you observe the television, the food on your plate, or the stars in the night sky. Without perspective, you wouldn't be able to see or notice anything. Because you have that perspective, you can also notice your thoughts. That's powerful, because it means you aren't what you think. Thoughts are part of you, but they aren't the whole you. Tuck that insight away and then apply it the next time thought monsters threaten to bump you off course.

Thought Labeling

Now we'd like you to do something with the thoughts you're watching. As you observe each thought, use this phrase: "I'm having the thought that...," and then briefly describe the thought. Here are a few examples to get you going:

- "I'm having the thought that I'll never make it through school."

- "I'm having the thought that I'm not smart and disciplined enough."

- "I'm having the thought that I really screwed up that report at work."

- "I'm having the thought that I may never finish this chapter on cognitive barriers."

- "I'm having the thought that this exercise is a little weird."

Keep this process up until the thoughts seem a little less important and compelling. They're merely ideas scuttling across your mind. They aren't real in the sense of the physical, material stuff of reality. They aren't a thing. They're literally *nothing*. They are phantasms— bridges that exist just long enough to get us to the next thought.

The Buddha discovered that thoughts become the source of suffering when we *believe* them—when we take them seriously and mistake them for what's real and true. Here's a quick thought exercise to help dispel that belief: Just thinking, "I am a lamp," will not brighten the darkness of a room, and it certainly won't turn you into a lamp! The simple process of labeling your thoughts will help you see them for what they are, just words produced by your mind.

We'd like you to go back to the white room and do one more thing: Bring to mind a valued choice, activity, or plan that sometimes gets blocked by negative thoughts. Visualize exactly what you'd do to actualize this plan. Once you have it, hold this image in your mind's eye and watch the thoughts that come up.

Let each thought move across the room, in through the left door and out through the right. Whenever you notice a thought about the possibility of something bad happening, label it a "danger" thought. Use the word "judgment" to label thoughts that evaluate or judge your plan, or even you as a person. Just watch your mind, noticing and labeling each thought about danger and each judgment. Then let the thought pass out of the room and notice the next thought.

Continue this process for four to five minutes, or until the thoughts begin to feel less important and compelling. Now look back. How many thoughts of danger did you have? How many judgments? Notice where your mind gravitates and how it reacts to your valued plans. Think of yourself as a fish, and notice where and when you're likely to get hooked.

Understanding this process is important. You can't change what your mind does—how it scares you or proclaims judgments—but you can feel less caught in it.

There's a name for what you just practiced. It's called *defusion*. Defusion is very much like what trained professionals do when they're called in to disarm a bomb, except here you're disarming your mind by revealing it for what it is and responding to it in a new way.

Once disarmed, your mind may try to feed you material that pushes you off track. But notice that defusion removes the charge, the spark and connections needed for your mind to go off and damage what matters to you. No matter how hard your mind tries, it cannot overpower a more defused stance.

Defusion is a powerful way to unhook yourself from your unhelpful thoughts. You get space. You become disentangled. You watch those mental goings-on until you begin to feel distance and perspective.

Defusion exercises, such as labeling your thoughts, help you make contact with two vital truths: that you are not your mind, and that thoughts are not reality. Your mind constructs ideas that sometimes help you and sometimes don't, but your mind isn't *you*. And the thoughts it creates are just that—thoughts. They are no more real than a daydream. Monsters they're not, unless we give them that power.

Using Repetition to Disarm Difficult Thoughts

You probably know the experience of seeing a neat magic trick or hearing a funny joke for the first time. But how about when it's repeated a second, third, or fourth time? With each repetition, the novelty wears off, interest fades, and we yawn. You can use this same dynamic to get some distance from your thoughts and feel less identified with them using a simple technique of repetition.

Edward Titchener, a pioneering psychologist in the early 1900s, discovered something unexpected about repetition. He noticed that if a person keeps saying the same thing between fifty and one hundred times, the words lose all meaning, and with that their power to disturb fades away. No matter how upsetting a thought might be when you start, it becomes blunted, almost silly, as you keep saying it over and over again.

Do it now and see what happens. You'll probably want to make sure you're by yourself, because most people will think you're nuts if they hear you doing what we're about to suggest you do. Take a particularly unsettling idea from the previous thought labeling exercise and distill it down to one or two key words. Then repeat those words out loud over and over again. Vary the pace and volume and keep going until the thought loses its impact and becomes a blurred, senseless string of sounds.

This simple technique is yet another way of teaching yourself that your thoughts are not you. They're just words that lose all authority when you create distance from them.

Seeing the Purpose of Cognitive Barriers and Thanking Your Mind

At some point, you've probably used a screwdriver to tighten a screw. If you're clever, you may have also used a screwdriver as a lever, or perhaps as a hammer to tap in a small nail. In each case you used a screwdriver, but its purpose or function depended on how you put it to use.

Thoughts can be like this too, acting sometimes as a hammer, other times as a kick in the pants, and other times as a gentle nudge. Or they can function like a noose, a ball and chain, or a net or web you can get caught in. Sometimes they might seem to tower before you like the Hoover Dam.

A good way to feel less hooked by your mind is to learn the *purpose* of your thoughts. What is a thought designed to make you do or feel? What function does it serve?

The list is long, and we can only begin to suggest the many functions here. Thoughts may serve to protect you from pain, remind you of your core identity, gear you up to do something, or scare you away from doing something else. Even painful thoughts have a function. Often their job is to protect you from an emotion or experience that's even worse. Whatever the purpose of a thought, you can bet it's arrived in your mind at that exact moment for a reason.

As far as values are concerned, you'll find that the functions of cognitive barriers can be lumped into two categories:

- To make you hesitate, feel scared, or withdraw so you won't do something

- To make you feel wrong, stupid, or foolish so you won't do something

That's it. The purpose of these thoughts is to fence you in so you won't take actions that are risky or difficult. The goal is paralysis. This awareness may be enough to give you the space to move forward when your mind says, "Be still. Do nothing." But if you continue and find yourself stuck, you can also weaken the blocking function of these thoughts by acknowledging your mind's efforts and thanking it. Here are a few examples:

- Thank you, mind, for trying to keep me from going back to school because I might fail.

- Thank you, mind, for telling me I'm too tired to spend time with my kids.

- Thank you, mind, for blabbing on about how selfish I am for wanting to backpack alone and pushing me not to.

- Thank you, mind, for claiming I'm not smart enough or good enough, that I'm unlovable, and that I can't live my life.

The point is to expose your mind's motives, to see what your mind wants you to do and why. Try this and see what happens. Right now, thank your mind for how it pushes you—often cleverly—to forgo your values, or even to put down this book.

Carrying Thoughts with You

Each time you step in a valued direction, particularly if it's new, thought monsters may visit you. Some will show up again and again. These old and familiar residents of your mind can seem heavy and unruly when packed between your ears—until you reveal them for what they are.

Go ahead and get some 3 by 5 index cards. Then take a card and write a blocking thought on it. Now look at the card. What do you see? Letters, ink, and words; that's it. That's your monster—letters and words. Do the same for another thought monster.

Once you've written a variety of these blocking thoughts down, notice that you can look at each thought on each card. You can hold each thought, too, right in the palm of your hand. You can observe and hold the monsters without becoming them.

You can do more, too. You can decide if you'd like to spend your time staring at the thought on each card or not. Do you really want to give it that much attention? Another possibility is that you could tuck the card away in your pocket and carry it with you as you go about your day. In fact, this is exactly what you should do. Carry the cards in your pocket at all times and add new thoughts as needed.

The point is this: Thought monsters that scare you with their predictions or deflate you with their evaluations are going to show up in your mind. You can't get rid of them. When you write them down, they become mere words, mere ideas, and you can relate to them differently. They're just letters and words on a card, with no more power than a piece of junk mail.

You can touch them and look at them without drowning in them. And whether or not you put them in your pocket, you carry them with you because they're a part of your life. That's exactly what these thoughts come down to: a part of life that shouldn't control or define you. You are more than what you think!

Exploring the Workability of Your Thoughts

Have you ever tried to type an e-mail while wearing mittens, mow your lawn with scissors, or drive your car to the grocery store with your eyes fixed entirely on the rearview mirror? You may laugh at the thought of doing any of these things. They aren't practical or useful, and they even sound a bit crazy. Thoughts can be like this too.

Cognitive scientists have estimated that each of us has about sixty thousand thoughts a day. Some are helpful, others not. Most of us don't tend to think of our thoughts this way. We think of them in terms of qualities like pleasant or unpleasant, good or bad. And we tend to pay attention to only a tiny fraction of them. Yet we often believe the thoughts we do pay attention to, and even when it's not helpful.

It can be empowering to stop and see that your thoughts need not be believed, trusted, or listened to. In fact, most of what we think can be parsed into the categories of helpful and unhelpful. Looking at it this way is a start. But don't stop there.

Ask whether your thoughts are helpful or unhelpful in terms of your purpose in life and moving in valued directions. This is what we're getting at in encouraging you to explore the "workability" of your thoughts—looking at whether your thoughts are helpful (or at least not harmful) when it comes to following your valued path.

With that in mind, think about what happens when you listen to your blocking thoughts and do what they tell you. Does that work? Do good things happen when your mind convinces you not to follow a valued path? Or does it feel like you're stuck trying to fill an Olympic-size swimming pool with an eyedropper?

Here's the bottom line: Does listening to your blocking thoughts—letting them stop you—help or hurt you? Look back and see. Think about some of the core values you've uncovered. Hone in on those you've had trouble turning into action. What thoughts got in the way? What was the outcome when you listened to those thoughts? How did *not* acting on your values impact your relationships, your work, your feelings about yourself, and other important aspects of your life?

You can find out right now by listing five blocking thoughts that steer you away from valued action. Put them down on paper.

Now go further. When you listen to these thoughts and do as they command, what happens to you and your life? What are the outcomes? Be specific.

Once you have it all down on paper or clearly in your mind's eye, you're ready to take stock. Are these thoughts working for you? Do you want to keep taking them seriously? Are you going to believe your thoughts, or your experience? Are you going to make decisions based on what your mind says, or the real outcomes in your life?

People have different reactions to this exercise. For Joyce it was a watershed moment. She wanted to start a science club in the middle school where she taught. Being a self-professed "science geek," she hoped to spark the kids' curiosity and interest them in scientific research. Yet every time she imagined taking steps to jump-start the club, her mind fed her blocking thoughts that stopped her dead in her tracks. Here are the five she listed:

- "It's going to take too much time and wear you out. Don't do it."

- "The kids won't be motivated. Don't do it."

- "The kids will just fool around and disappoint you. Why bother?"

- "Other science teachers will be angry because they'll look bad for not initiating something like this. Just leave it alone."

- "It will be a nightmare getting approval. It will be too difficult. You can't handle it."

Each thought replayed over and over again, and when Joyce listened, she ended up doing nothing. Doing nothing gave her some short-term relief: She felt less anxious. After all, not going forward with her dream meant she didn't have to face the challenges and potential pitfalls of starting the club.

But eventually the relief was overrun by feelings that were even more troubling than anxiety. Joyce felt listless, worn-out, and defeated. As she dug into this a bit more, she turned her attention to the workability of her blocking thoughts. As she did, she noticed other outcomes that were bad, too:

- Feeling guilty for letting the kids down

- Feeling sad because I see kids with real interest and no place to explore it

- Feeling down on myself for not doing something that's important to me

- Feeling a little burned-out, like I'm just going through the motions with my job

- Feeling bored after school, with nothing interesting to do in the afternoon

After wading through this process, Joyce became clear about one thing: Her mind wasn't working for her; it was working against her. In fact, listening to her blocking thoughts was costing her big-time in the form of sadness, guilt, and loss of meaning. Worse, she wasn't doing what mattered to her. "Workability" became her new mantra.

Finding Refuge in Present-Moment Awareness

One of the best ways to deal with painful thoughts is to take refuge in the present moment. This is where you are anyway. The present moment is also the only place where you can act to make a difference in your life.

But as it turns out, the mind doesn't like the present moment all that much. The mind is like a time machine that continuously launches us into a future that's yet to be or a past that's now over and unchangeable. In fact, this is exactly what most blocking thoughts do. Some propel us into the future: Something bad will happen, you'll fail, you'll feel bad about yourself, and so on. The rest of the mental blocks focus on the past, recycling missed opportunities, regrets, and painful moments that seemingly robbed us of what we would need to go forward now.

As you move ahead with a valued goal, here are three specific ways to soften the impact of blocking thoughts as you stay in the now: using your senses to be in the moment, mindful breathing, and thought releasing.

Use Your Five Senses to Be in the Moment

Move from your mind and its preoccupation with worries about the future or ruminations about the past to your present experience. Notice what each of your senses is telling you right now, wherever you are.

Spend ten to twenty seconds noticing what you see: shapes, colors, patterns, and so on. Then observe the sounds you hear: voices, street noise, wind, the hum of the refrigerator—whatever you hear. Now shift to your nose and try to identify any specific smells. Next is taste: Are there lingering impressions from a meal, or any subtle tastes in your mouth? Finally, attend to your sense of touch. Feel where the world presses against you: your feet against the floor, your body against a chair. Feel any sense of texture, pressure, or temperature. Also notice sensations *inside* your body.

You can do this simple practice almost anytime and anywhere. It shouldn't take more than two minutes, yet in that brief time it can deliver you from thoughts of danger and judgment to the safety and richness of the present moment.

Mindful Breathing

Your breath is another good place to go when your mind is full of warnings and judgments. Your breath is always with you—always available. And when you focus on your breath, it will bring you back to the present moment time and time again.

Mindful breathing is nothing more than bringing your awareness back to your breath, as often as necessary, with intention and purpose. Here's how to do it in three simple steps:

1. Notice every part of your breath: the feeling as the air is drawn in through your nostrils, the coolness in the back of your throat, the sense of your ribs expanding, then the release in your diaphragm as you exhale. Don't try to breathe in any specific way; just watch all of this as your breath becomes the center of focus.

2. As you inhale, silently say "in" to yourself, and as you exhale, silently say "out." Or if you like, you can count each breath up to ten, and then start over.

3. Throughout, your mind will naturally wander out of the present moment. After all, that's what minds do. When that happens (and it will happen), don't get frustrated or berate yourself; look at it as an opportunity to practice coming back to the present. When thoughts intrude, just notice them, let them go, and gently bring your attention back to your breath.

As you practice mindful breathing, be aware that even the most proficient meditators—even those cloistered far away from the buzz of worldly distractions—experience distracting thoughts. When they notice the mind jumping around, they don't worry about it. What they do, and what we're asking you to do, is to notice that and then simply steer attention back to some part of the breath.

This is a skill, and like any skill it takes some practice. It's best to start small. Find a quiet place and do mindful breathing for two to three minutes at first. Then work your way up to longer periods in your quiet place, or just about anywhere you find yourself.

Studies have shown that two twenty-minute daily sessions of mindful breathing are a sufficient "dose" to relax your nervous system and significantly improve mood. We recommend that you work your way up to that over time.

Thought Releasing

Some of our thoughts are sticky. It's like they're coated with superglue: Once they enter the mind, we can't seem to let them go. Other thoughts seem to hang together like strings of sausages, each thought linked to the next, and the next, on and on, forming a long chain of negative associations. Cognitive barriers that stand in the way of your values often show up in one of these forms. You get stuck on one that won't seem to let go, or they just keep coming at you, one after another.

The best way to counter sticky thoughts or sausagelike thoughts is with thought releasing. We want to be clear that this isn't a way of suppressing or stopping thoughts. Both tactics are essentially impossible anyway, at least in the long term. In thought releasing, what you do is acknowledge the presence of a troubling thought and then *let it go* without getting more involved with it.

In a way, you do exactly the same thing when you go walking. To walk, you have to let go of one step before you can stride into the next, and so on. Thought releasing is like that. You let go of each thought so your awareness can keep moving and flowing.

There are many ways to go about releasing thoughts. Here we'll offer three that many people find helpful. The first is a variation of a strategy we covered already. You simply thank your mind for each thought. Notice what you're thinking, thank your mind for this thought (and all thoughts your mind produces to protect and guide you), then inhale deeply, filling your lungs. As you release the air slowly, imagine the thought drifting away as you empty the air from your lungs. Do this for a minute or two to open clogged mental arteries.

A second thought releasing strategy is to picture your thoughts as leaves on a stream. As each thought comes into awareness, imagine putting it on a leaf in a stream that's flowing along at a moderate pace. Then just watch it drift around a bend and out of sight. Do the same with the next thought. Keep up the visualization until you feel less stuck and have more distance from the thoughts your mind is offering you.

This exercise can take many forms. Some people find it easier to visualize placing thoughts on helium balloons and then watching them as they drift away on a breezy day. Or you might place your thoughts on Frisbees and watch as they sail out of sight. You could do the same thing with cars, clouds crossing the sky, or just about anything you can imagine coming and then going, passing in and out of your awareness. Be creative and choose something that resonates with you. All you need to do is attach your thought to a moving object and watch it as it disappears. Then wait for the next thought and do the same. Just notice and let go.

A third form of thought releasing involves opening your hand. The strategy for this technique is to use a physical gesture of release as you let each thought go. When a thought comes into awareness, observe it for a moment and then open your hand as if you were freeing a captured dove. This gesture—of both surrender and letting go—parallels the opening of your mind so you can move on to the next moment and whatever awareness it brings.

Your Thoughts at a Distance

We're all blessed with a human mind, and subject to its constant thinking. We don't have to treat every thought it proffers so seriously. We don't have to act on its advice when our experience tells us that the advice is limiting, unhelpful, and self-defeating. All of the techniques you've learned in this chapter will help you contact this basic truth.

You don't need to change the contents of your mind. You don't need to change what you think. You need to change your relationship with your mind and its infinite products. Your mind is a word machine that keeps coming up with thoughts whether you want them or not, and whether they are useful or not. It will keep this up until the day you die.

You have two choices here. One is to get hooked into thinking that you are your mind, and that every thought reflects reality. With this choice, you'll be stuck in a futile attempt to think differently before you can live differently. This will keep you from acting on your valued intentions.

Or you can accept these thoughts and be willing to take them along for the ride. You can observe them with equanimity while pushing ahead with what matters. With this approach, there is nothing to be fixed or changed. All you need to do is watch, accept, and distance yourself from mental chatter as you move toward what matters to you.

Chapter 9

Willingness with Emotional Barriers

Let's not forget that the little emotions are the great captains of our lives and we obey them without realizing it.

—Vincent van Gogh

Emotions are celebrated and repressed, analyzed and medicated, adored and ignored—but rarely, if ever, are they honored.

—Karla McLaren

The first step toward change is acceptance. Once you accept yourself, you open the door to change. That's all you have to do. Change is not something you do, it's something you allow.

—Will Garcia

E motions color just about everything we do. We can relish them, be haunted by them, fear them, or cling to them. Like the weather, they morph and change, varying in power, strength, and impact. They can leave us feeling more alive, or feeling torn apart and wounded. They can be our best teacher or our worst enemy, our greatest asset or an Achilles' heel. It all depends on what we do with them.

Emotions Have a Purpose—Helpful, Wise, and Dark

While we know a great deal about emotions, much more remains unknown. That said, one thing is clear: Emotions happen to us and despite us. They're not something we do or create without significant help from our environment, disease, chemical substances, and an array of other influences, including our good old mind.

You can get a sense of that right now by trying to make yourself as happy as you know how to be. Don't try to do it by thinking about something you enjoy. Just flip your happy switch. Difficult? You bet. We can't do it either. Nobody has that kind of switch. Emotions happen, often outside our control.

Their main reason for existence is to help us survive. They mobilize our bodies to take action when faced with threat to life and limb. Danger ignites feelings of anxiety and fear, which can mobilize us to fight or flee. Anger sparks self-defense. Even sadness may play a protective role by offering us a time to pause, reflect, and heal so that we can go on.

Even pleasant emotions protect us. Love and joy help us form meaningful bonds, prompting us to connect, care, reach out to others, and give and receive support. Infants need this from their mothers, especially in their earliest days and months. There are many emotions that are adaptive in this sense. In all cases, they focus your mind and energy on a response that protects your life and well-being and helps you grow.

A second function of emotions is to alert us to the intuitive inner wisdom that knows what's right for us. Feelings of relief, love, contentment, and even guilt can awaken us to what we value and help us press on in a direction that matters. This is also why it hurts when we lose something that matters to us, including our values. Emotional pain is one way our bodies tell us that something mattered enough to care about losing it. Using our emotions wisely also strengthens us against impulses that might damage or defeat the good in our lives.

But as you probably know, there's also a dark side to emotions. Instead of signals we can use wisely to point us in a direction, they can become sources of chronic pain. Instead of supporting valued choices, they can drive us to run away from things that matter, and even run away from life itself. Fear is the usual culprit: fear of failure, fear of shame or embarrassment, fear of loss or rejection, fear of feeling alone or empty. We are, in short, afraid of pain.

When we explored barriers to valued living in chapter 7, the fear of pain emerged as a huge obstacle to doing what matters. That's not just physical pain; we mean any unpleasant emotion that hurts.

Sooner or later, moving in almost any valued direction will stir up a difficult emotion—a feeling we'd rather avoid. The more we fear emotional pain, the greater our temptation to turn away from what we care about. Over time, it's almost as if the fear gets pasted right up against our values. When the fear wins, our lives tend to lose.

Whether you're learning a new skill and facing discouragement or seeking to hear and understand your partner despite feeling hurt, much of the time doing what you value will have some cost. To keep going, to keep doing what you care about, can require staying with feelings you're almost desperate to be rid of.

Clearly, learning to face difficult emotions is crucial for living a valued life. But there are at least three other reasons why facing emotions is important to your well-being: The unknown feeds fear and keeps it alive. What we resist tends to stick around. And what you avoid controls you.

The Unknown Feeds Fear and Keeps It Alive

What you resist you cannot know—and what you don't know, you will fear. Emotions have a natural life span. Like a wave, they surge, crest, and then recede.

If you have a tendency to avoid painful feelings, trying to numb out or somehow shut off the hurt, you may not appreciate that painful emotions have a limited life span. As pain wells up, you may cut it off before seeing that there is a crest, and beyond it a downward slope. You may not know that even the worst emotions subside—naturally and spontaneously.

Try sticking with an emotion and watching it to see how this works. With time, you'll learn something about how long they last, and how they morph and soften over time. Without this knowledge, you'll remain stuck in a pattern of fleeing or avoiding strong emotions.

What We Resist Tends to Stick Around

The more you resist your emotions, the longer they'll last. Every attempt to suppress a feeling just keeps it alive and simmering in you. Even worse, the emotion may intensify, gathering steam as if you had put a lid on a pressure cooker.

Researchers have studied this phenomenon in depth, and this large body of work points to one conclusion: Pushing away unpleasant emotions doesn't work. In fact, it backfires. You get more of the very feelings you'd rather not feel, and in situations where you'd rather not feel them. Interestingly, it doesn't work the same way for positive feelings. Trying to not be happy when you're happy won't make you happier. In fact, it'll kill it.

This idea is hard to get, let alone accept, because it conflicts with just about everything we've learned about emotions since kindergarten: the importance of being in control and the perils of feeling discomfort. So think of it this way: The dynamic we're getting at here is something like trying to put your hand over the open end of a garden hose with the water turned on full blast. Imagine that the water represents painful feelings you'd rather not feel, and they're flowing out of the nozzle in a relentless and powerful stream. You can't control the spigot, so you do what seems like the next best thing: You use the palm of your hand to try to cap off the flow.

If you did this with a garden hose, you'd find that the pressure builds and builds and builds. At some point, it will find a way out, and you'll get soaked. Other things and people around you will get wet too. Your well-intentioned efforts to shut off pain end up creating a big mess in your life. These are the costs of suppression.

What You Avoid Controls You

The more you avoid emotions, the more they control you. When you're dead set on not having a particular feeling—hurt, embarrassment, anxiety, loneliness, or anything really—your choices and reactions are all about getting away from it. You strategize, you cope, and you try to arrange things so that you never have to face that emotion. Any situation or choice that might trigger the feeling must be avoided.

In these situations, if you take the time to notice, you'll probably see that your mind is getting into the mix, too. And if you observe closely, you'll find that many of the situations that trigger avoidance of emotions are linked to your values. In fact, values are major triggers for painful feelings. Because of the pain these situations create, your mind tells you to avoid them. The problem is, when you do, you avoid living a valued life too.

So here's the paradox: To control an emotion, you give up control of your life. The opposite is also true: Every time you face an emotion, it becomes less scary and overwhelming and exerts less control over you. So, how to resolve the paradox?

You won't do it by thinking. Emotions flow from the most primitive centers of the brain. Those centers don't respond well to our mind and our rational side. It's like trying to argue with a lizard. It won't get you anywhere.

You need to go to the roots with this one—right down to your experience. Instead of running away, you get present with what you feel. Instead of shutting down, open up to it. Instead of trying to control it, let it be.

Ways of Staying with Your Feelings

The rest of this chapter will give you three ways to stay with your feelings. Each method will strengthen you and prepare you to bring the emotion monsters onto your bus so you can keep heading in valued directions. The first, and perhaps most important, skill is emotional contact. We'll outline this approach at length, then we'll also discuss positive outcome imagery and radical acceptance and give you techniques for practicing those, as well.

Emotional Contact

When you make full contact with something, you touch it, open up to it, and experience it as best you can. Like right now, you're contacting this book, opening up to its content, and taking it in. In this moment, you're also in contact with many other aspects of your environment and experience, like the textures of the pages, the lighting and temperature in your surroundings, and your mood and how you're feeling physically. You already have plenty of practice contacting people and objects in your world. You can learn to do the same with your emotional life.

The beauty of emotional contact is that it helps you get used to difficult emotions a little at a time. In a way, it's like a toddler learning to take those first steps. We've all been through that. It's a huge challenge. Yet with practice and hard work, lurching and falling starts to look like one step, and then another. Teetering steps turn into graceful walking, and sooner or later, we do it unconsciously. Walking becomes second nature.

One Step at a Time

Experiencing a difficult feeling can be approached in small, gradual steps too. With each step, you get closer to knowing what it's like to feel what you feel, what it's like to be who you are and get present with the emotions you're experiencing. In this gradual way, you learn to go into the emotions where you'd normally pull away. Over time, a sense of being overwhelmed is supplanted by a deepening emotional intelligence—an awareness of the flow and rhythm of your moods.

Begin by going back and reviewing the values you've uncovered while working with this book. Focus on values you care about deeply and struggle to turn into action. These are areas where living your values is obstructed by barriers. Then imagine enacting each blocked value until you notice a value that triggers an emotion you'd like to avoid. This is the value you'll start with.

Bring that emotionally blocked value into your mind's eye and visualize a situation where acting on that value would trigger a difficult emotion. Bring the scene to life as vividly as you can. Where are you? Notice all of the details of your environment. See who's present and what's being said.

Continue to watch the scene slowly evolve, as if it's being projected onto a movie screen one frame at a time. As the events unfold, pay attention to your feelings: hurt, anger, shame, sadness, and especially fear. As the scene plays itself out, find words to describe what you feel, and then put them on paper. Notice the strength of your feelings. Notice any impulse to escape or push them away. Be aware of any desire to retreat from your valued actions in this situation.

Amy, a new librarian, went through this exercise because she was tired of letting her emotion monsters control her life. She looked at her core values with an eye to those mired in emotional blocks and found that inspiring children to learn was a place where this was happening. So she imagined enacting that value by organizing story groups for pre-readers. As she watched the scene slowly unfold, she noticed that the head librarian was playing a leading role in the drama. He's biding his time until he retires and resists any new initiatives.

Amy saw herself making a request for resources to do the new children's groups, but in her mind, this appeal ignited an angry exchange with the head librarian. As Amy settled into that, she began to see that she was deathly afraid of anger, conflict, and feeling judged. Not asking was Amy's way of avoiding fear, and her fear of fear kept her from acting on her values.

Having words for your feelings is important. When Amy imagined the scene with her boss, she wrote down the following description of what she felt: "I feel threatened, scared he'll attack me and call me naive. I have this feeling of danger, as if something really bad is going to happen. I think he has contempt for me, and that gives me the feeling of being bad or wrong."

Neutralize Fear by Feeling It

Now that you've zeroed in on the feeling you don't want to feel, the feeling that stops you from doing what matters, how can you lose your fear of this emotion? The answer is to feel it—a little at a time.

Start by finding a moment in your past where this difficult emotion was prominent. Think back over the years to such a time, and when you find one, visualize it as fully as you can. Where were you, who were you with, and what were you doing? As you imagine the scene, see if you can really make contact with the feeling. Notice how you experience it in your body. Do it slowly.

Now describe the emotion. Find the words that fit what you feel and repeat them silently to yourself. Notice any impulses that go with the feeling and describe them too. For Amy, the words were "frightened" and "worthless," and the impulses were to apologize and run. She used those urges as a gentle reminder to do the opposite: to go in a bit when her history was compelling her to pull back. That's important with urges or tendencies. Try to do the opposite of what you'd normally do, one step at a time.

Just keep describing the feeling to yourself, and as you sit with the emotion, find words for any change in intensity. If other feelings start to weave their way into the experience, find words for them too. Notice thoughts and urges that go with the feeling and label them, prefacing each with "I'm having the thought that..." or "I'm feeling the urge to..."

Let your feelings do whatever they do. If they feel stronger as you ride up the wave, that's fine. Just watch and describe what happens. If the feeling changes into something a little different, notice and describe that. You can also describe your feelings in ways that are more symbolic: Think of a color, shape, or texture that fits the feeling. Or think of a sound or temperature that seems to capture the essence of the feeling.

Meet each old urge or habitual behavior with a response that goes against the grain. When the urge is to pull back, go in. When the urge is to freeze, move. When the urge is to frown, smile. When the old pattern is to remain mute, speak. When the urge is to explode in an angry tirade, be still and silent.

Keep going for four to five minutes, silently talking to yourself the entire time. And when you've reached that time limit, let it all go—the images, the words, the emotions, everything. Take a deep breath and bring to mind a scene where you feel truly at peace. Any peaceful memory will do. Just bask in this image while breathing slowly and deeply.

Once you've relaxed, reflect on what you learned about yourself. Do you notice anything that seems new or different? Is there anything in your experience that you absolutely cannot have, cannot feel, or cannot think? Look around the edges for any sticky spots, name them, and be mindful of them the next time you practice. By "sticky," we mean those times when your mind proclaims, "It's not working," "You can't do it," or "You're not really going to do it, are you?" Remind yourself that this is a process that will change you over time. But you need to make time for that change.

You'll get the most out of this exercise if you repeat it several times. So do that. Imagine everything again, describe your emotions, and counter any urges with opposing action. Keep at it for four to five minutes and watch for changes in the intensity and quality of the feeling. Then release everything with some deep breaths, and picture your peaceful scene.

Cycle through emotional contact and relaxation several times in a row. After a few repetitions, you'll notice that the target emotion doesn't seem to upset you quite so much. This desensitization effect is exactly what you're looking for. The more time you spend with this exercise, the more desensitization you're likely to achieve. As your body and mind start to get used to experiencing "difficult" emotions, they will lose their power to steer you off course.

A Word of Caution

With enough emotional contact, the emotion may go away, or it may transform into an entirely different experience. View this as a potential positive side effect, not the goal. It isn't a good idea to practice emotional contact just to feel better. This is a slippery slope. If you do this exercise just to be more comfortable, there will be times when you won't feel that way. And then what? You're right back where you started, and perhaps feeling more defeated.

The point of emotional contact is to develop a new relationship with your mind and emotional life. When you consciously choose this path, you're doing something radically different than you've done before. This opens up the possibility of getting something new in your life.

You're doing something else, too. You're learning that your emotions aren't enemies and that you can have them just as they are, even the painful ones. And you're doing this for a purpose. This isn't just about feeling bad or being comfortable. It's about finding a way to feel what you feel and think what you think *and* do what matters to you. It's about your life.

You have lots of freedom in how you do this exercise. If you want, you can increase the amount of time you contact your emotional barriers. You can push it up to eight, ten, or fifteen minutes, or even more. You can vary the setting by practicing at home, in a park, in your car, or on a plane. You can even vary the depth of the imagery, starting small and then going into it more deeply.

But here's what you can't do: You can't hold back from the experience. Regardless of how you do this exercise, you must choose to be willing to open up to whatever you think and feel for however

159

long you're practicing emotional contact. Anything else is conditional. If you attach conditions to the exercise, then you might find that you'll do it, but only if it doesn't get too difficult. If you do stop when it gets too difficult, that's conditional.

Another way to think about it is like this: Suppose you really wanted to go swimming. Swimming without conditions would mean jumping right into the water. You just go for it. If you make swimming conditional, you might slowly wade into the pool to see if the water is warm enough. If it's too cold, you don't swim. With this exercise, we're asking you to go ahead and jump into the pool of your experience, because your life is important to you.

So whatever you decide, be sure you're doing it with your arms wide open, willing to embrace the experience with your life in mind.

Shorthand Steps for Emotional Contact

Here, in shorthand form, are the basic steps of emotional contact so you can easily refer to them. Remember to start with willingness, and don't forget that the purpose of this exercise is larger than the monsters—it's about your life!

1. Vividly imagine the scene where valued living is blocked by an emotional barrier, and observe your feelings.

2. Notice how the emotion connected to the scene is experienced in your body.

3. Describe the emotion to yourself in as much detail as possible.

4. Describe the impulses that go with the feeling.

5. Do the opposite of what the urges, thoughts, and feelings compel you to do.

6. Watch the emotional wave, describing as it increases or diminishes in intensity.

7. Give the emotion a shape, size, color, texture, sound, or temperature. Describe all of this in words as you observe the feeling.

8. Notice and describe thoughts that go with the feeling.

9. Notice other feelings that enter the experience or how the first feeling transforms.

10. At the end of four to five minutes, let go, breathe deeply, and visualize a relaxing scene.

11. Repeat this process until you begin to feel a desensitization effect.

12. Reflect on what you've learned about yourself and your emotions.

Amy used this approach to get at the roots of her fear of fear. She brought to mind a very old confrontation with her dad—one of those painful memories that most of us never forget and that we wish had never happened.

When she was fourteen, she had a crush on a boy at school. She asked her dad if she could go out with him, and her dad's response was explosive anger, filled with expletives, demeaning comments, and innuendos about her sexuality and self-worth. As she relived the scene, the emotion of feeling worthless grew to a disturbing level. This is how Amy described the experience to herself as she did the exercise:

> *I feel small, shrunken. I am nothing, without value.*
> *It feels like a hot pressure on my chest, hard and crushing.*
> *It's getting bigger, a huge, gray blob. Pressing, pressing. I*
> *want to escape it, but I'm going to go in. Now I feel the*
> *sadness—despair really—that I'll never be alright. Always*
> *wrong, always stupid, always wanting the wrong thing...*
> *The sadness is bigger than the worthless feeling...not so much*
> *pressure, but now the feeling seems stuck to me like tar.*
> *Hopeless, dark. I want to get away from it, but know*

I should lean in. Stay with it, open to it. The worthless feeling is much smaller now, almost lost in the sadness. Much less... I want to drink, to laugh hysterically—anything to stop the sadness. Thinking about the TV show Seinfeld *and George Costanza's line "Do the opposite, baby!" Coming back to the feeling. I'm having the thought that there's nothing funny about this. And I have the thought it will never end, like the empty black universe just going out and out... Now I feel oddly lighter, a strange emptiness that's almost like relief. Like letting go and drifting.*

When time was up, Amy took a slow, deep breath. She imagined a meadow she had played in with her brother when they were little, rolling and rolling in the grass.

Once you've achieved some desensitization, imagine the valued behavior you've been avoiding. If the painful emotion comes up, follow the steps outlined above to weaken its chokehold over you. Stay with the feeling and describe to yourself every part of the experience. Keep at it until the feeling diminishes or begins to shift to something else.

The keys are observing without running away; finding words for every detail of the experience, particularly as it changes; doing the opposite of old habits, urges, and impulses; and reflecting on what you learned. Do that and you'll create a new relationship with yourself, your emotions, and your life.

Positive Outcome Imagery

When painful feelings block us again and again, it's easy to focus on the negatives. It's as if we're being programmed and reprogrammed again and again with more bad news. This programming can become our mantra: that everything is bleak and dark, and nothing will ever change.

The way to break out of this cycle is to reprogram your mind and body. You do that by focusing on the *positive* outcomes of living your values. You sink into the sweetness of living out your intentions. You can start right now. We offer you two techniques for doing this. In the first, you develop a clear picture of the rewards that may come from acting on a particular value. In the second, you'll envision a success story in which you act on your values, even if emotional barriers show up.

Get in Touch with the Rewards

Choose a value of yours, perhaps the one you worked with in the emotional contact exercise. Once you have it in mind, see yourself enacting your value just as you wish. Nothing stands in your way. You're free of barriers and successful in doing what you set out to do.

Descend into the beauty of this moment, this experience, like you might linger while watching a beautiful sunset. What does success feel like on the inside? Notice any emotions and physical sensations. See if you can touch a sense of satisfaction or purpose, a sense that what's happening matters.

Stay with this image, and when you're ready, slowly shift your attention to the world around you—the people, events, and environment that surround you in the imagined scenario. What's different? Become aware of how people in the situation are reacting to you and to what you've accomplished. How does it feel to have surmounted an old barrier? How does it feel to freely do something you've been afraid to pursue? Notice how the situation changes for the better because of what you did in the service of your values.

Stay with this exercise for as long as you wish. When you're ready to wrap up, write down all of the positive outcomes you discovered during the exercise. Let them serve as a reminder of what is possible.

Amy used this exercise to connect with the many good things that would follow from honoring her values. She imagined two scenes. In one, she saw herself presenting her proposal to the head librarian with heartfelt conviction and steadfast resolve. As she made her case, she felt powerful and effective. She had a sense of mission, a greater purpose. She imagined that the old guy tried to put her off, but she kept at him until the story groups happened.

In the second scene, she pictured herself being with the kids at the library as she led the first story group for pre-readers. She saw the eager faces all looking at her, caught in the thrall of a great tale. And as she touched that, she felt an almost electric joy, a sense of doing something useful, even important. She saw how her actions were like pebbles she was dropping, and how the ripples she was creating enriched the lives of those eager young children.

When she'd finished the visualization, Amy wrote down all of the positive outcomes she could imagine, for herself and the kids, and even for her community.

Create a Success Story

By creating a success story visualization, you can increase your confidence and motivation to act on your values. The focus of this type of positive outcome imagery is on what you'd do and feel during a values-driven event where emotional barriers might show up. Before doing a success story visualization, write out the sequence in advance so you know exactly where you're going. Use this sequence to construct your visualization:

1. Begin with the very first thing you say or do that starts you in the valued direction. See your action; hear your words.

2. See and hear how others respond to you.

3. Observe the emotions that come up, especially those that tend to block you from taking valued actions.

4. Watch your feelings without resistance, even if they're scary and unpleasant. Remind yourself that an emotion is like a wave, and sooner or later it will crest and recede.

5. See yourself completing what you set out to do. Imagine all of the positive outcomes, as you did in the previous visualization. Don't skimp on this. Bask in every good thing that happens, for you, for others, and for your world.

Notice that a success story visualization isn't just about success. It's about having a clear intention, facing the emotional pain that might show up in that situation, and reaping the rewards of sticking with your valued intention in the face of obstacles.

When you're ready to begin, relax with a few deep breaths and do a body scan to note and release any physical tension. Then do the complete success story visualization four to five times so it will fully take root. Repetition will help you increase your certainty that you can deal with negative feelings. It will also strengthen the connections between valued behavior and positive rewards even before you've actually engaged in the behavior out there in the real world.

Amy decided to give the success story visualization a try. Here's what she came up with for the narrative:

> *I'm in the head librarian's office. It seems dark. He's leaning back in his creaky swivel chair. I start to tell him about the advantages of pre-reader story groups—how they excite kids about books, and how the books are chosen to teach important life lessons. He isn't looking at me, and I start thinking that this is stupid and worthless, that I'm stupid and worthless.*
>
> *"We need your time for other things," he says. He looks down at his hands as if the discussion is over. He's so not interested. I feel almost sick with the worthless feeling, but I'm not going to stop. I keep standing there, repeating my points. Now the "stupid" thought and uncomfortable feeling are joined by something else: a feeling of my power, my purpose. I won't take no for an answer, I'm certain of it. He makes me feel stupid, but I persist and eventually he gives in and agrees.*
>
> *Now I can see the kids in a circle, excited and listening. I'm reading* The Little Engine That Could, *teaching them about perseverance. They're taking it all in and hanging on every word. I feel joy, this electric excitement all through me. I feel relief that I'm finally doing what I'm supposed to do. I'm so happy looking at the children's rapt faces.*

Radical Acceptance

Your stance in regard to your emotions—whether you stand with or against them—matters a great deal. Emotions themselves aren't barriers. They only function that way when we think pain isn't normal—that it's really bad, unacceptable, and ought to be avoided. This leaves us in opposition to genuine aspects of our experience. Emotional barriers are built with this kind of mortar. This drives us to think, say, and do things that ultimately bring more pain to ourselves and to those we love. We've given you two ways to tear down these barriers by staying with your feelings (emotional contact and positive outcome imagery). A third way is a different approach, radical acceptance.

Radical Acceptance Gives You Freedom to Be You

Radical acceptance is based on an open and honest appraisal of life. Early in this book we said that life is hard. But suppose that it isn't inherently hard, and we just make it hard.

Suppose that the deeply ingrained instinct to recoil and avoid actually makes things worse and turns the pain of life into agonizing suffering. Instead of doing what matters—heading in the valued direction with firm resolve—we steer around the monsters, making turn after turn until we become lost in the ennui of a directionless life. We aren't really driving the bus anymore; we've become listless passengers on a bus going nowhere. The fear we give in to when we rush away from pain gradually becomes depression due to a life not fully lived, a life we've lost control of.

So, what are we to do, then? Well, we can start by getting honest about a couple of things. The first is this: Pain is an inevitable and unavoidable part of life. There's no escaping that truth. The collective wisdom passed down over generations, balanced with strong research evidence, tells us as much.

The second pearl of wisdom that we must come to terms with is this: Our efforts to avoid pain are what make life hard, not the presence of pain itself. This is an old idea too, but one that has been confirmed by research. Avoiding pain inside our skin increases suffering and pulls us out of our lives.

These simple truths point to a solution in radical acceptance. With radical acceptance, we watch pain come and go without resisting it or trying to control it. It flows from our willingness to develop a new relationship with our pain and hardships.

We can't be truly free—free to live by our own lights, our own values—without radical acceptance. Nelson Mandela spent twenty-six years in South African jails because he had *chosen* to do what mattered—for himself and his country. No one could stop him. In that choice, and despite decades of confinement and loneliness, he was free. Because he was able to accept the pain, Mandela was liberated to *be* his values, to be the embodiment of resistance to apartheid.

Viktor Frankl, an Austrian neurologist and psychiatrist, describes a similar choice in his book *Man's Search for Meaning*. He was imprisoned in several concentration camps during World War II, and often attended to the medical needs of others, despite having almost no medical supplies. Frankl had an opportunity to escape, but he chose to stay in the camp, imprisoned along with his patients. He experienced that moment as the freest and most peaceful in his life. He'd chosen to accept whatever pain, whatever fate awaited him, in order to do what mattered. In the end, he concluded that the meaning of life is found in every moment of living, no matter how painful or desolate. Life never ceases to have meaning, even in suffering and death.

In this day and age, we tend to take a different approach to pain. The cultural expectation seems to be that emotional pain can and should be avoided. Indeed, we're seen as failures at life if we experience significant sadness, fear, or shame. We're encouraged to fix our pain: cheer up, cope, take a pill, take more pills. The message from almost all quarters—from TV, from advertising, and often from our families and friends—is that pain is bad, we shouldn't have to tolerate it, and we're defective if we experience it. This culture of feel-goodism has delivered nothing but empty promises.

The trouble is, this cultural message is wrong—and it's bad for us. Pain is part of the fabric of life. Philosophers, theologians, scholars, and scientists much wiser than us have made this point clear. But we forget that basic truth and miss the point that pain is absolutely necessary if we are to live our values.

While most of us won't have to brave imprisonment in order to do what matters, on some level we face the same choices as Frankl and Mandela. At times, we'll have to choose to experience emotional pain if we are to live our values, successfully navigate values conflicts, and create a life worth living. As we make each valued choice, we must accept the feelings that go with it.

Radical acceptance my seem abstract or hard to grasp. To help make it more concrete, here are the key points to keep in mind:

- Difficult feelings are a necessary part of your life and living your values.

- What you feel now is exactly what you should be feeling, given your history and whatever you're doing or not doing.

- Feelings just are—they don't need to be judged.

- Feelings don't have to be fixed or controlled, just observed like a wave that will soon vanish into a sandy shoreline.

- Difficult emotions are a teacher, pointing out what matters enough in your life to hurt for.

- Accepting pain gives you the freedom to do what matters and dignifies the effort you put into living your life.

Exercise for Radical Acceptance

Go back to the work you did in chapters 3 and 4 and examine your self-growth and service values once again. Look to those where you're stuck, unable to turn your good intentions into values-consistent actions. Then list two values in each category, for a total of four values you'd like to act on more often and regularly. For each value, bring to mind a specific situation or relationship in which you'd like to bring it to life. This will take you beyond mere ideas to something more concrete.

Now, just as you did in the exercise for emotional contact, visualize the scene and notice any difficult feelings that come up. This time there's no need to describe your emotions; just practice radical acceptance. How? All you need to do here is simply observe the emotion just as it is. Your mind will judge the emotion if it feels "unpleasant" (which itself is a judgment), so just notice that and say, "Judgment; there's judgment." Then return to the emotion and let whatever you feel and sense be what it is. Take a deep breath and see what happens to the tension in your body. Just observe it.

As you're observing and noticing like an explorer might do, ask yourself if there's anything in this emotion that you really cannot, must not have. See if you'd be willing to feel what you're feeling if that meant you'd get to live out your values.

What you feel and think is there for a reason, calling out to you that this thing, this value, matters enough for you to care, to hurt about it, to feel strongly about it. Open up to it—in your mind and heart, and even physically. Make a gesture of widening your arms as if you're about to hug a long-lost friend. Maybe it's possible to embrace the pain because feeling it frees you to do things you've avoided or turned away from.

Keep up your deep breathing. Stay with the feelings for another minute or two, and as you end the visualization, say to yourself, "I accept and feel whatever I need to feel." Open your arms one more time as a symbolic gesture of openness to your history and your experience.

Now repeat this exercise with the three other values and situations you identified. It won't take more than fifteen minutes, and it's well worth the time. Each time you practice the art of acceptance, you're doing something profoundly good for yourself and your life.

Taking the Emotion Monsters with You

As you can see, emotional barriers to doing what matters aren't something we can avoid or get around in the long run; they aren't challenges we can numb away or defeat with willpower. These difficult emotions are experiences we must take with us as we go in valued directions, because we can never truly slay these emotion monsters. But we can learn to tame them and put them in their proper place.

Taking them with us means carrying them lightly—letting the experience come and go, rise and fall, not pushing it away, and not holding on to it either. Pain is our birthright, our teacher, the source of our humanity, and sometimes the source of our nobility. And whatever we might wish, it's along for our whole journey.

Franklin D. Roosevelt rallied the United States around this very idea during the Great Depression. During his first inaugural address, he said, "The only thing we have to fear is fear itself—nameless, unreasoning, unjustified terror which paralyzes needed efforts to convert retreat into advance." This timeless message is dead-on.

When you allow fear to drive your choices, you'll end up doing nothing. You'll be too afraid to take a bold step or even a small one, too afraid to speak out against injustice. You may even end up in a state of inertia, seldom accomplishing anything that has true meaning for you.

This may creep up on you over time, until you reach the end of your life and wonder what happened—so many dreams left unfulfilled. Where did the time go?

Most of us will reach that place of reflection at some point, often right before we die. If we allow fear to run our lives, then the moments we spend reflecting on our lives may be quite dark. We may end up thinking that we never accomplished anything that would have meant something to us. We may even feel that it was all for naught, that life was a big waste of time. Sadly, in that moment we'll also see the high price we paid for letting our fears control us. But by then, it's too late to do much about it.

It doesn't have to be this way. The antidote to fear is to face it, open to it, and embrace it for what it is: an emotion, a teacher, a friend, and a reminder that what you want in life matters enough to feel strongly about it.

Chapter 10

Willingness with Behavioral Barriers

Life is a process of becoming, a combination of states we have to go through. Where people fail is that they wish to elect a state and remain in it. This is a kind of death.

—Anaïs Nin

We all have dreams. But in order to make dreams into reality, it takes an awful lot of determination, dedication, self-discipline, and effort.

—Jesse Owens

The life you have led doesn't need to be the only life you have.

—Anna Quindlen

The dawning of a new year is celebrated around the world. It's a time to take stock and reflect about the past year and look forward to the year to come. Amidst the revelry, horns, fireworks, and one too many drinks, the turning of the calendar makes us pause. We look to this brief moment in time as an opportunity to make changes in our lives, to do things differently, perhaps to make amends.

We make resolutions. You've probably made them too: "This year I'll spend more time with family and loved ones, lose weight and get in shape, eat right, quit smoking, enjoy life more, get out of debt, learn something new, get more organized, help others in need..." The list is endless. Anything can be the target of a resolution. You may even resolve not to make them.

Despite good intentions, most of us fail to keep our resolutions. We get stuck when it comes to turning our resolve into clear intentions linked with actions. We run up against behavioral barriers, like lack of knowledge, skills, or resources. When we don't find a way forward, our resolutions become a long series of broken promises and unfulfilled expectations. You can't afford to do that with your values. Your life is on the line.

Types of Behavioral Barriers

The good news is, you can overcome behavioral barriers. But first you need to get clear on what they are, so let's start there. Behavioral barriers to living a valued life can take many forms, but all of them can be distilled into four general themes. We'll take a look at each of these to see how willingness can help you overcome them:

- A failure to specify the steps that will take you in a valued direction

- Inadequate knowledge

- Weak or underdeveloped skills

- Logistical issues, such as time, distance, finances, and so on

Specifying the Steps: Moving from Vague to Specific

The hope, the intention, and even the determination to act on your values won't be enough. You need a step-by-step plan for doing so. Focusing on a general goal or direction often results in getting stuck. That's because you can easily lose motivation when you face big, complex tasks, or even just intentions that are vague and nonspecific.

Think of it this way: Your values are like compass bearings, and goals act as mileposts along the way. Sometimes when you get in the thick of things, you can't see distant landmarks. Taking it step-by-step and having small, short-term goals will keep you moving in the right direction even when you lose sight of the big picture

If you don't know exactly what you want to do and how it would look out there in the world, it's hard to take steps in any direction. For example, Scott has the intention to listen openly and nondefensively to his wife every day. This is a great intention, but it may never actually happen. It's hard to commit to doing something so vague. It's like saying, "I'm going to eat better." What does that mean? Scott needs to make the intention specific.

So the first thing you need to do is to establish some concrete goals. What will you do to carry out your intention, and when, where, and how will you do it? To answer that, imagine watching yourself behave in a way that's consistent with your intentions. What are you doing with your mouth, hands, and feet? What do you see as you watch yourself taking action? Get specific and write it down.

Going back to Scott's example, in terms of listening openly he might ask two key questions: "How would my wife know that I'm listening openly?" and "What would listening openly look like?" If he answers these questions with specific and concrete goals in mind, he might end up with something like this: "I'll face my wife, look into her eyes as she speaks, and give her my undivided attention. I'll do that each night when she talks about her day. I'll also ask her questions about her day to show my interest. And when she's unhappy about an issue in our relationship, I'll listen carefully and ask questions."

Let's apply the same guidelines to his second intention: being nondefensive. In this case, a specific action might look like "The next time my wife complains that I don't help with the kids, I'll listen and ask questions about what I can do, without saying, 'Yes, but...,' offering retorts, or seeding an argument with harsh words."

Can you see the difference between vague and concrete? Specific and clearly spelled out goals have a far better chance of being turned into action. That's the easy part. But it isn't enough.

Along with specific goals, you need a specific commitment to take a step, or a leap. In Scott's case, it might sound like "I promise myself that I'll listen to my wife describe her day this evening, and that I'll ask questions about it." You may have to make these commitments anew each day until your valued behavior becomes a habit. Start each day with a goal and a commitment to that goal and see how it goes.

Here's an example to make this process crystal clear. Anthony hopes to get a contractor's license. He has strong values about building well-made family homes. One day he hopes to use his talents to help families in need of low-income housing. This is his intention.

This is a complex endeavor, and the mere intention to build low-income housing probably won't suffice. He has to get specific and think in terms of concrete steps that, if followed, would take him toward doing what he values. Here's what Anthony came up with:

1. Get a job as a site foreman.

    a. Write a résumé covering my work history.

    b. Apply to at least two contractors a week in a widening geographic area.

2. While collecting required hours, enroll in courses toward licensure.

3. Collect recommendations.

4. Sign up and take the licensing test.

5. As a licensed contractor, bid on remodeling jobs and build a nest egg.

6. Buy a lot and build a family home on spec.

7. Learn about low-income housing developers.

8. Find a partner for a small project.

In drafting this list Anthony was making progress, but there was one more thing he had to do. To turn his intention into action, he had to make a time-and-place commitment to the first step of his goal. Anthony did just that.

He decided to buy a résumé writing guidebook by the end of the week and have a first draft of his résumé done by Sunday night. This concrete goal was very doable in the short term, and by Sunday night he'd accomplished the first step. He was already moving in a valued direction and acting on his intention. As he continued working his way down his list, he felt more empowered with each decision and each action. Doing work he valued seemed not just possible, but within his grasp.

Lacking Knowledge and Skills

Having knowledge and skills enable so much in life. It's easy to miss that, taking what we know or can do for granted. We may fail to see the potholes in our understanding and competence that require attention so that we can move smoothly in a valued direction.

And it turns out that knowledge may not be enough; you also need know-how—the skills to do something smoothly and efficiently. You probably know this firsthand if you've learned to ride a bicycle. Chances are you didn't learn by reading about bicycle riding, the mechanics of bicycles, the function of various muscles, or what have you. You did it by getting on a bike, wobbling, falling, and, eventually, riding. Without that experience, you just can't ride. The fact is, you need direct experience and practice to become skillful at just about anything.

Aidan, a twelve year-old, learned this lesson the hard way. He loved watching the X Games and knew the name of every snowboard trick there was. He dreamt of one day being like Olympic gold medalist Shaun White, doing gravity-defying Double McTwist 1260s. So his parents set him up with lessons, and once he got the hang of it on the bunny hill, he was ready for the big time—or so he thought.

He lined himself up to tackle the half-pipe, thinking he'd just do a Backside 180. He knew what that trick looked like and could tell you each required step. But when it came down to it, the only move he made was a face plant, leaving him banged up and deflated. Aidan had knowledge, but he hadn't yet developed the skills he needed to do what he set out to do.

Aidan's experience is common. And it turns out that most behavioral blocks standing between us and our valued choices come back to one of two things: We either lack crucial knowledge or information, or lack the skills we need to follow through. Like Aidan, sometimes we have the knowledge, but not the skill. Other times, we have the skills but no idea how to use them. This can manifest in any number of ways:

- You want to stop fighting with your kids but don't know how to create appropriate rewards and consequences.

- You want to speak out and address issues in your community but don't know how to organize your thoughts for public speaking.

- Your mother needs help with financial decisions, but you have no idea what to do.

- You yearn to make music but don't even know how to read music, let alone play an instrument.

- You want the intimacy you once had in your sexual relationship but don't know how to get it back.

- You're a talented artist but have no idea how to make a living with your art.

177

Gathering Information and Acquiring Knowledge

Being informed is enormously useful with many life decisions, whether buying a car or home, moving to a new neighborhood, traveling to a foreign country, or expanding your horizons and interests. As you gather information you acquire knowledge, and both can help you avoid buying a lemon—or making unwise choices about how to live your values.

In fact, gathering information and gaining knowledge may be a pivotal first step before you can move in a valued direction. Yet actually doing so can feel like a huge barrier. You may not know where to begin. If that sounds like you, then start by making a commitment to this first step: figuring out what knowledge you need and where you can find it.

All you're doing here is making a commitment to taking a concrete step toward finding out what the options are. You can find information in many places, but don't neglect what you can learn from other people, especially people you trust who seem to know what they're doing. Their success is a model for your own success. They can help you get going in good directions more quickly than would probably happen if you were going it alone. This is a wise use of your time and energy.

The next move is to show up wherever you decide to get the knowledge and training you need. If you're trying to master public speaking, you might attend a Toastmasters meeting. If you want to learn to budget your money and invest wisely, you may take a class, sit in on a seminar, or consult with a parent, friend, or financial advisor. Exploring your musical interests may point you to a music teacher who can help you find an instrument you'd like to learn. Or if you're keen on enriching the intimacy in your marriage, you may read a book on hot monogamy or find a therapist to help you sort out your relationship issues.

Sometimes getting the knowledge you need isn't so easy or clearcut. You may have to face feelings of vulnerability. It can be hard to admit that you lack knowledge about something that really matters to you, and embarrassing to seek help. On a more practical level, financial costs or time limitations may get in your way.

Right now, the important thing is to commit to learning what you need to know, despite any emotional barriers and regardless of how much time or effort it may take. Ask yourself if you're willing to learn no matter what, and then answer with a resounding yes! That's what Anna Mae did.

Anna Mae is a costume designer for a regional theater company, but her real passion is playwriting, which she's dabbled in since high school. When she showed some scenes she'd written to the director of the theater, he told her she needed some basic training in playwriting conventions and to work on her dialogue.

The feedback sent her into an emotional nosedive, and Anna Mae stayed stuck there for six months. Then she realized that she needed to get more training or give up her dream of writing altogether. She looked into her heart and knew she wasn't willing to let go of her dream.

So Anna Mae searched for a playwriting class at local colleges, but none was available. She thought about taking an online course or reading books on the subject, but she decided that she really wanted to work directly with a teacher. So she wrote to the Screenwriters Federation for ideas. They suggested someone who tutors budding playwrights for a fee. It turned out the training wasn't cheap, but Anna Mae signed up because it seemed like her best bet for becoming a better writer.

Strengthening Your Skills

As you saw with Aidan, having lots of knowledge about something is a far cry from being able to do it effectively. To hone skills, you have to practice them. It isn't enough to read a book, watch others, or take a class; you have to apply what you learn.

Knowledge may breed confidence, but it doesn't necessarily breed competence. Practice gives you both. You also need willingness— willingness to keep at it despite the inevitable failures and feelings of discouragement. Despite that face plant, Aidan kept up his practice and eventually mastered some difficult snowboarding tricks.

So many things in life are like that. We have to pull ourselves back up, dust off, and go at it again and again. Take cooking, for instance. If you want to improve your culinary skills so you can bring people together around interesting meals, reading a book by Julia Child may be a good start, but it's not going to turn you into a gourmet chef. You'll need to practice a lot of recipes—and sometimes botch them. But if you stick with it, you'll become confident and skillful in delivering a great meal. Many skills are like that. We need to be willing to fall on our face to acquire the skills to live out our dreams.

Of course, nobody likes to fall. We'd all rather be skipping along, unscathed, unembarrassed, and proficient. But there's no way to acquire mastery without going through the trouble, effort, and tears that come with learning a new skill.

There's no sugarcoating this point. Mastery and success don't happen overnight. They take hard work, and you have to keep your eyes on the prize, not the difficulty of getting there. This is true of gaining the skills you need to live your values, and it's also true in the bigger picture: living a valued life.

When you focus on the difficulty and disappointment, you're likely to give up on strengthening your skills. You'll settle for being less effective than you could be. That's a detour into the land of mediocrity—an odd place filled with halfhearted gestures, untapped potential, and dreams that are realized only partially, at best. Just think about that.

Imagine that you're very ill and need to see a doctor. In the land of mediocrity, all you'll find are second-rate physicians. Go further. In this land, you'll also find halfhearted teachers, indifferent musicians, uninspired artists, and disengaged parents, partners, and friends. In the land of mediocrity, everyone is confined to living on the fence, never to know their true potential. This is what happens if we're unwilling to take the trouble and make the effort needed to maximize our skill, potential, and effectiveness. But you don't have to live there.

Using Covert Rehearsal to Build Your Skillfulness

Willingness is the key to keeping out of the land of mediocrity—willingness to try, and try, and try again. Real-life practice is the most effective way to get better at doing most things. But if something feels too risky or overwhelming, an effective way to get started is to do covert rehearsal. This involves practicing a new skill using visualization. You've already used this technique to face cognitive and emotional barriers. Now you can apply it to behavioral barriers.

Start by listing specific steps, or mini events, necessary to become proficient at your new skill. Also include a few moments where problems may show up and how you can respond to them.

Here's an example of the covert rehearsal list Amanda came up with. She wants to develop assertiveness skills. She sees this as being helpful for living out many of her valued intentions. In this case, it can help her advocate for changes at work that would be meaningful for her values around family and parenting:

1. I approach my boss in the morning about making an appointment to discuss our health insurance.

2. I notice that I'm nervous and take a deep breath as I'm talking to him.

3. Before the meeting, I again notice that I'm nervous. I take some deep breaths. I focus on my goal of getting health coverage for my children.

4. I make my request in a clear, calm voice. I address expected additional costs for the company (giving the numbers) by suggesting that workers with children could share the costs.

5. I imagine my boss objecting or (based on previous experience) putting the whole thing off as an issue for the board of directors. I see him looking grim.

6. I take a deep breath and remember my kids. I ask what percentage of the extra costs workers would have to pay to make this reasonable for the company. My voice is clear and calm; my posture's straight.

7. My boss stares at his desk and says he doesn't know.

8. I take a deep breath and remember my kids. I ask if he'd bring a formal request from me (and signed by other workers who are parents) to the board.

9. My boss reluctantly agrees, and I say I'll give him the request by a specific date.

10. As I walk out of the office, I feel a sense of accomplishment. I feel proud of myself for standing up for my kids. When I get to my desk, I tell my friend June, and she congratulates me. I feel like I've done something good for my family today.

Go back and reread Amanda's last step. Notice something important about it: She imagines something positive as a reward for her great effort, and it isn't trivial. She sees the link with her values. Also notice that the rehearsal sequence isn't all roses. Amanda feels nervous several times, and her boss resists her. For each obstacle, Amanda includes a centering response (deep breaths) and refocuses on her value. Before Amanda took the real-life step of confronting her boss, she visualized the entire sequence ten times—until she had enough practice that she felt more confident and relaxed.

If you want to use covert rehearsal to practice new skills, here is a review of the process:

1. Set a clear, values-based goal of the skill you'd like to use and manifest by your actions.

2. Write down each mini step of the visualization, just like Amanda did, including problems and points where the situation could be stressful. Also include some kind of centering

or relaxing response for these moments of stress, as well as a brief statement to reconnect you to the value at stake here. Don't be afraid to have plenty of mini steps built into your visualization. They make the rehearsal seem more realistic.

3. Remember to include a last step where you feel good about yourself and perhaps get some other reward for your efforts. Link the goodness of this moment with your values.

4. Choose a quiet place to do your visualized rehearsal. Before you begin, get centered and relaxed. Do a few minutes of mindful breathing or mindfulness of your five senses (see chapter 8) to help you settle into a calm state.

5. Take some time to visualize the environment of the first step of your sequence. Where are you? Who else is there? Place yourself in the setting.

6. Slowly and deliberately visualize each step of your rehearsal sequence. As you imagine taking a deep breath in response to stress, actually do it, and also be sure to recall the value you're enacting.

7. Repeat the covert rehearsal visualization until you feel calm and confident about using your new skill to do something good for yourself and your values. Now you can take this skill into real life.

Overcoming Logistical Issues

Some behavioral barriers to enacting values are actually logistical issues, such as time, money, distance, resources, the needs of others, and so on. These problems often feel defeating because they don't yield easily to our intentions, or even our hard work. Sometimes it seems there's no clear course, no path without an obstacle, and this can be overwhelming, even if you have a great deal of determination.

Good Old-Fashioned Problem Solving

The answer to logistical blocks can often be found in problem solving. That term is undoubtedly familiar, and you've probably used a wide variety of problem solving techniques in your life. Here's a formalized and well-established technique that we recommend. It involves seven steps:

1. Identify the goal you want to reach.

2. Brainstorm alternative solutions. There are a few rules for brainstorming: No criticism of ideas. All ideas are welcome, no matter how freewheeling, crazy, or wild. Come up with a lot of ideas; fifteen or more would be best.

3. Narrow down the list by eliminating unlikely alternatives. Also consider combining options.

4. Evaluate the remaining options to find the best choices. For each likely alternative, list its positive and negative consequences, both short term and long term, and list the positive and negative impacts on you and others.

5. Based on your analysis and keeping your values in mind, choose the best option.

6. Outline the steps for implementing your chosen solution and commit to the first step.

7. Set a time to evaluate the outcome. While all of your thoughts on the matter are fresh, also consider selecting a backup option to pursue if the first one doesn't work out.

Let's examine each of these steps using Paul's example. He's a collector of African-American quilts. He has a passion for the amazing and unique artistry of black quilt makers and wants to show his quilts across the United States so that he can share that passion with other people. He'd like to launch a traveling museum exhibit but doesn't have the financial resources to do so.

Early on, Paul learned that this venture wasn't going to be easy. Each museum required a personal visit, with sample quilts and a slide presentation, before making any commitment to hosting an exhibit. The trouble was, he didn't have the money to spend weeks on the road talking to curators. Here's how he used problem solving to overcome this barrier:

1. **Identify the goal.** Paul needed to raise $6,000 (plus living expenses while he took a leave from his job) to make a personal presentation to eight target museums.

2. **Brainstorm alternative solutions.** Paul and a friend did a half-hour brainstorming session and came up with about twenty ideas, some of them admittedly far-fetched.

3. **Narrow down the list.** Of the ideas they came up with, these were the six best, most likely, or most practical solutions:

   a. Sell some of his quilts.

   b. Borrow the money from his aunt.

   c. Get a loan against his quilt collection.

   d. Do a fundraiser with friends.

   e. Ask museums for travel funds.

   f. Delay the project for a year so he could save enough money.

4. **Evaluate the remaining options to find the best choice.** Paul analyzed the six alternatives in step 3. It took some time, but because turning his dream into a reality was important to him, he considered it time well spent.

5. **Choose one of the options.** Paul's analysis left him feeling that the benefits of borrowing from his aunt outweighed the risks. Below, we've provided his analysis for that option, to help you see how he arrived at that decision.

6. **Outline the steps and commit to the first step.** This was simple because the only action required was for Paul to talk with his aunt. He'd already done the estimating work to know how much money he'd need. The hard part was committing himself to the conversation, because his aunt was prickly and her responses hard to predict. Paul realized he had to be willing to accept whatever she said or did in the service of his valued project.

7. **Set a time to evaluate the outcome, and choose a backup plan.** The time frame for evaluating this option was also straightforward; Paul would know if this solution was workable as soon as he had his aunt's reply. Since the outcome hinged on his aunt's decision, Paul went ahead and chose a backup plan. If his aunt said no, he'd sell some quilts to finance the project. While this was definitely a second choice, it seemed more viable than his remaining options.

	Positive Outcomes	**Negative Outcomes**
Short-term	*I'll get the money quickly.* *I'll see the curators soon.*	*The conversation with my aunt will be awkward.*
Long-term	*I may get my traveling exhibit rolling in less than a year.*	*I'll owe money.* *I'll feel obligated to my aunt.*
How it affects me	*I'm excited to get started.* *I'll get recognition for my collection.*	*I'll feel embarrassed if it takes a while to pay my aunt back.*
How it affects others	*Thousands of museum goers will get to see the creativity of the African-American community.* *I'll bring others joy and excitement about this work.*	*None.*

Some people may see this type of problem solving as a mechanical process. But it works very well if you add in commitment to the entire process. First, you need to commit to doing all of the steps, to walking through each one. It can take some effort to examine all of the alternatives, and it may even raise some anxiety. Some options will have disadvantages, but you *will* find the best choice.

Next, as always, you need commitment to take action. You need the willingness to face whatever stress, effort, or negative outcomes arise on your path to valued living.

Using Your Time Wisely

One of the most common logistical blocks people experience is a perceived lack of time. How often have you said or heard someone else say something like "I want to do [whatever], but I just don't have the time for it" or "There aren't enough hours in the day."

Whenever you hear yourself saying or thinking something like this, stop. We really mean that: Stop. Don't just blindly accept this thought as gospel truth. These thoughts about time are a great setup for giving up on doing what matters to you. Chances are, you've taken that bait more than once. We know we have.

Time is always there to be used as you wish. And how you use your time matters. When you perceive that you don't have enough time, the usual culprit is failing to use your time wisely—failing to set priorities. When people feel squeezed for time, it usually means they're giving too much priority—and time—to activities that aren't really meaningful to them.

So look at how you're using your time. Pick a day and do an inventory of how you're spending your coin of time. Once you have it all down, look at each activity and ask yourself this: "Does this serve a value of mine or not?" Count up the activities that are values-based and those that are not. Then compare the two numbers.

If the number of values-based activities is smaller than the other number, you're not using your time as wisely as you could. We're not saying you should be balanced—and we're not about to tell you how you should use your time. We're just saying that your time should be full of values-oriented activities. If not, you're likely feel burned-out and frustrated over *time*.

You also might find it helpful to go back to chapter 6, where we suggested ways to prioritize your time and activities based on your values. And don't forget to be watchful for procrastination and foul compromises.

Navigating Behavioral Obstacles Is Important

Life is all in the doing. Yet it can be difficult to get moving. Sometimes we want the easy way out, but that's a dead-end street. It doesn't lead to values-based living. To deal with behavioral barriers, you need to keep your destination in mind and define clear steps for getting there.

You also need knowledge and information, and you need the skills. Mickey Mantle didn't make it into the Baseball Hall of Fame by just knowing how the game of baseball is played. He had to get out there and practice, practice, practice. It takes plain old hard work to live your dreams.

Sometimes knowledge without skills can undermine your best intentions. The school of hard knocks offers an education that can be shortchanged by advice and scads of information. This is exactly what happened to an emperor moth when a well-intentioned woman tried to "save" it.

One day when Julie was out in her backyard, she found the cocoon of an emperor moth. She took it inside so that she could watch the moth emerge from its confines.

On the day a small opening appeared, she sat and watched the moth's progress for several hours. The moth struggled to force its body through that little hole, then it seemed to stop making progress. It appeared as if it had gotten as far as it could and could go no farther. It just seemed to be stuck.

Then Julie, in her kindness, decided to help the moth. So she took out a pair of scissors and carefully snipped a wider opening.

The moth emerged easily, but it had a swollen body and small, shriveled wings.

Julie continued to watch the moth, thinking that at any moment the wings would expand and be able to support the body, which would contract in time. She had read a bit about what happens when emperor moths break free. Yet her experience was not like what the books described. Instead of emerging and flying, the poor moth spent the rest of its short life crawling around with a swollen body and shriveled wings. It wasn't able to fly.

What Julie didn't understand was this: In order for the moth to fly, it needed to push its way out of the restricting cocoon. The painful struggle through the tiny opening served a cause. It was necessary to force fluid from the moth's body into its wings so it would be ready for flight once it achieved its freedom from the cocoon. Freedom and flight could come only after painful struggle. By depriving the moth of struggle, Julie unwittingly deprived the moth of health and its natural purpose in life.

You may see a bit of yourself in this story, particularly in how you might wish to move through life without behavioral barriers. The story also hints at another possibility, one that may seem a bit wacky at first: Could it be that your behavioral blocks aren't your enemy? Is it possible that you need to struggle to "force fluid from your body into your wings," that you need to feel some pain in order to have the kind of life you so desperately want?

We're not suggesting that you can just take off and fly into a happy life. All we're asking is that you consider that life challenges are necessary for you to grow and to fly.

Chapter 11

Living Your Life on Purpose

Two roads diverged in a wood, and I, I took the one less traveled by,
And that has made all the difference.

—Robert Frost, "The Road Not Taken"

Life's journey is not to arrive at the grave safely, in a well-preserved
body, but rather to skid in sideways, totally worn out, shouting "holy
shit, what a ride!"

—George Carlin

For of all sad words of tongue or pen, The saddest are these: "It might
have been."

—John Greenleaf Whittier

Your life isn't a series of accidents. Everything you've done and everything you've experienced up until now has gotten you to exactly this place, this moment in time. And it's from here that you look forward. The question is, forward to what?

The answer hinges on you. Your choices, your intentions, and your actions create your destiny. Will the rest of your life be one replay after the next of what came before? Or will you act to create a life of value and purpose with the days you have left? Nobody can make this choice for you. You'll have to decide.

If you want to get something new, you need to do something new. It's that simple. You need to make a commitment to doing what matters before the final curtain call. This is how you take charge of your life. Everything in this book has been about that. Only you can live your life on purpose. The time is now.

Getting Yourself Moving

There's no big secret to how you create a values-driven life. You can't think your way into a life of purpose, and you can't feel your way into it either. Beliefs won't get you there, and neither will intentions or strong motivations. You need to take action. You need to get yourself moving. You need to do something with your mouth, your hands, and your feet. That's it.

Even if you're willing to invite the monsters onto your life bus— willing to take on the fear, the risk, and all of the barriers—you still need to do something. You still need to put the bus in gear and steer toward what matters. What you do is what you'll be remembered for, like it or not. And what you do is a reflection of what you value, like it or not.

If you're willing to set your course in a valued direction, start with a commitment. The commitment isn't that you'll always be perfect. Nobody can live up to that. And the commitment isn't that you'll always achieve every goal or get what you want. That's an impossible dream. The commitment isn't even that you'll never break your commitments! We all fall short once in a while. The commitment is simply to use what you've learned in this book to go forward in new, potentially more vital ways as best as you know how.

Are you willing to make that commitment? Are you willing to risk doing something new in order to create something new in your life? This is a yes or no deal; you really can't do it halfway. You may have to start each day with a reminder about your commitments. And as you do, watch your mind trying to get you to play it safe. Minds love the familiar, even if it's bad for us.

Sure, making a commitment to do something new is risky. You don't know what may happen. But think about the risk of doing more of the same. If something hasn't been getting you closer to what matters in your life, then doing more of that seems like a huge risk—and a fairly predictable one, at that. You pretty much know what you'll get, and it isn't more of what you want.

So, right now, ask yourself if you're willing to do something new. Say it out loud. Write it down. Tell someone about it. Ask others to support you on your new path as you take one bold step after another.

You may have to meet each second of the day with your commitment, taking thousands of tiny persistent steps throughout the day, or you might take a giant leap here and there. Either way, it starts with that first step. If you made a commitment just now, then you just took a step in the service of your life. That's profound.

Honoring Your Commitments

You're the only one who can stand up for your life. When you honor your commitments to following through on valued intentions, you're taking a stand. You're making your values a priority, first with intentions, and then by following through. When you fail to honor these commitments, you won't be living your life.

The commitment we're asking you to make is saying yes to your values and yes to the inevitable pain. It means taking responsibility for your life. That's big, and it's important. And we mean "responsibility" in all senses of the word. After all, responsibility means that you always have the *ability to respond*, wherever you find yourself in the pond of life.

You have a great deal of response-*ability* in how you use your hands, feet, and mouth—what you create, where you go, and what you say. You have response-*ability* in the choices you make, the intentions you craft, and the commitments you keep. You also have response-*ability* in how you respond to the barriers you face on your journey. Will you meet them with willingness and acceptance, or with white-knuckled resistance?

Assuming you're on board with willingness, you need to start somewhere. A life on purpose isn't something you discover and then that's the end of it. It's something you create by turning your response-*ability* into purposeful actions that matter, and then doing that again and again. Let's take a look at some approaches that can help you do just that.

Set Goals That a Living Person Can Do

If you were going to climb a mountain, or just walk down a gentle path to the ocean, you'd have to take one step after another to get there. You'd have to move. You'd have to take action and do something. This is exactly what you should do when setting goals that support your values: Say, "I will," and then take a step. These are goals of the best kind.

The analogy of climbing a mountain reveals something about what makes a good goal: It needs to be something that a living person could do. And it needs to move you in space and time and in a direction toward one or more of your values.

Think verbs, like studying, reading, walking, loving, caring, working, playing, or praying. A living person can do these things. A living person can lend a helping hand, share a gift, go to a place of worship and pray. A living person can eat a salad, go for a run, meditate, read to his or her children, dance, perform musical theater, and so much more.

Also think adverbs: compassionately, skillfully, thoughtfully, respectfully, lovingly, confidently, diplomatically, dazzlingly, vitally, zealously, wisely, willingly. *How* do you want to be as you take action in service of your values? We can face adversity openly or combatively. We can persist with challenges resolutely or not at all.

When you focus on the verbs and adverbs, what you'll notice is that you can't buy any of them. They can't be lost, depleted, or stolen. They're choices. The capacity to do these things lies within all of us. They can be used or ignored, embraced or forgotten. It's up to you. Just remember that there are certain things that any living person can do, no matter what the circumstances. We all have an infinite capacity to show kindness and love toward others and ourselves, rather than adopting reactive anger and bitterness as our guiding credo.

The goals you set can be baby steps or giant leaps. If you take a leap, or even a small step, and it doesn't seem to work out, you can always break it down into smaller, more specific steps that are easier to do. Like learning a complex dance routine or a new skill, you may have to break larger goals down into bite-size chunks. They're more easily digested that way, and less overwhelming. We've given you some ideas about how to do this in chapter 10, on facing behavioral barriers.

You can also use imagery to check to see whether you're setting goals that you can do. Imagine that you're performing your life on stage. You have a value in mind, and you have several goals or steps you'd like to take in that direction. You're committed, ready, and willing. Your task here is quite simple. You just need to show the audience that you've acted on one of your goals, that you've taken a step in a valued direction.

What would you do to show them? And as you take a step, would the audience know you're doing what you set out to do? If the answer is no, you've probably set a dead person's goal.

Avoid Dead Person Goals

Let's set a different stage. It's opening night at the Life Theater. The Dead Players, a four-person theater group known for their creative monologues and stand-up routines, are about to go on. It's the first night of the tour, and media pundits are saying it's a must-see. The show is sold-out, and you can sense the crowd's wild anticipation. You find your seat. It's curtain time.

David is the first act. He struts out on the life stage with a goal clearly in sight. He'll show the audience how he stops smoking. The audience falls silent, gripped by anticipation. Minutes pass with no movement or action. And when David takes his bow, all he gets is boos and hisses.

Evelyn is next, hoping to reveal a nuanced performance of her goal: being less anxious. Standing motionless, as if fixed in space and time, Evelyn practices her art. The audience stares blankly, waiting for something to signal the start or end of it all. When Evelyn finishes, a heckler shouts, "I paid good money for *this*?"

Adrianne follows right after, and she's thinking she can turn the audience's mood around. Her routine is complex: worry less and be more confident. She adopts the pose of a mannequin. The silence in the audience is deafening. As she bows, she notices that folks are getting up to leave.

Dustin is the last to go on—the closing act, the grand finale. His routine is a neat number on understanding himself better and waiting for the right time to change. He's silent and peaceful throughout his routine, and so is the theater. By this time, everyone has left. The rest of the tour is cancelled after opening night.

The moral of this story is simple. Each performer set goals that a dead person could do just as well as a living person. Nobody in the audience could tell they were doing what they set out to do. That's the trouble with dead person's goals. They involve no movement, no action. You won't be able to tell that you've achieved them, and neither will anyone else. For that reason, they won't benefit you or your life.

If that seems a little abstract, here are some signals that can alert you that you're setting dead person goals:

- Your goal focuses on achieving something that is completely inside you, like feeling happy, less depressed, less empty, more confident, more worthy, or more peaceful.

- Your goal involves stopping a behavior (talking, hitting, yelling, thinking, drinking...) without adding something in to fill the gap, preferably an alternative, more constructive, "will-do" behavior based in your values.

- Your goal is delayed; you're procrastinating or putting it off until you're older, until the "right" time, or until things change.

- You're turning your life over to metaphorical ideas and symbolism, thinking you just need to somehow absorb, transcend, digest, understand, figure out, or fix something about yourself.

Avoid setting goals that fall into the categories on this list. The problem with applying these sorts of goals to yourself and your life is that there's no way to know you've achieved them. Instead, think like an actor (but not a Dead Player!). Acting is all about movement, expression, and engagement—and a valued life is just the same. Living person goals get you going, and if they're rooted in your values, they will take you forward. Going forward means some kind of change: doing less of one thing and more of another, or stopping one behavior and doing something else instead. The key word here is "and."

Even if your values around health lead you to decide to quit smoking, you need to build in activities you will do instead, something healthy or vital to replace smoking and keep you moving in the direction of better health. Or if you choose to cut back on your work hours, you need to find another purpose for that extra time. If working less is in the service of a value, how can you fill those hours with activities that lead you in the direction of that value? The point is that you are doing, not behaving like one of the Dead Players. That's how to create a life worthy of a standing ovation.

The Three-Day Rule

Everything in life is constantly changing. This is a basic truth. Your body is changing. Your experiences are changing. Time is always marching forward. Each day is new, though it may seem like more of the same old, same old. Nothing ever remains the same.

Living your life on purpose is based on this basic idea. Everything is always changing, and you can change too, in this very moment. But change can be hard. We know that living your life on purpose is difficult. People find it hard to get moving and try new things. To do so, we have to overcome the inertia created by our old habits, our minds, our judgments, and our histories.

Here's something we also know: If you commit to a change and act on it for at least three days, the change will start to become a habit. Like a ball moving downhill, you gain speed and momentum. And if the new habit expresses your values, it will start to become part of your life. But you need to give it three days. You must be unwavering during this time, steadfast in honoring your commitment to do something new and vital that speaks to your values.

You can apply the three-day rule to any of your self-growth or service values. Select a value that you'd like to nurture more. Make a commitment to move it from the realm of ideas into clear intentions, and then come up with specific actions that will embody those intentions. What could you do right now to bring this value of yours to life? Pick something you could repeat for three days. You don't have to repeat it constantly for those three days, but you do have to engage in this action consciously on a daily basis.

Once you have what you'd like to do in mind, remind yourself of it. Post a note on your fridge or program a reminder on your cell phone. It's also helpful to tell someone else what you've committed to doing. Promise yourself that for three days you'll follow through on this one step in service to one of your values. After the three days are up, pause and reflect. During those three days, what was it like when you put values into action? Sink into the sweetness of it.

Carrie used the three-day rule to support her health values. She'd been struggling with her weight and exercise while juggling family responsibilities and a full-time job. There never seemed to be time to take care of herself, and when she did try to do something to get herself in shape, her efforts were always fleeting. It was always one step forward, three steps back, or so it seemed.

Carrie decided to apply the three-day rule. She focused on exercise, specifically walking. Her days were full, but how she used her time was not formed in cement. There were cracks in her routine. When she took an honest look at it, Carrie found that there were windows of opportunity where she could build walking into her day.

She zeroed in on her lunch hour and committed to walking twenty minutes during that time. She did that for three days. When she paused to reflect on the fourth day, she realized that she was feeling better. No, she hadn't dropped any of her extra pounds during the first three days; she knew that weight doesn't just fall off like that. But beyond feeling physically better, she felt good about doing something for herself—something that mattered.

Those three days soon became three weeks, and then three months. Now she's walking forty-five minutes during her lunch hour, and some of her friends at work have decided to join in. Over that time, she's come to see that taking the time to walk has had benefits beyond her health. She has more energy for other things in her life, including her five very active kids. Exercise has also become a meaningful way to connect with her friends at work. One small step had a large impact.

You can do the same with just about any value. Just be sure not to bite off too much at once. Start with one step—something you can do every day for three days. Be patient and kind with yourself. There's no speedometer glued on your head with any of this. Choose the steps and the pace that will work for you, and make adjustments as you go along. With each step, you'll build momentum. As your actions in regard to one intention take hold, you can turn your attention to other values and intentions and apply the same principle.

This is exactly what Lars did to nurture his listless relationship with his wife, Annie. Both of them led very hectic lifestyles and felt depleted. They spent time together in the evenings, but both of them were usually exhausted and in their own worlds. They didn't share much. Mostly they joined together to eat, camped out on the couch watching news and killing time before bed. At least they shared that.

They had become like two ships passing in the night, each with its own sense of purpose, but without a common connection. This gulf was weighing heavily on Lars. Considering his values in the context of his marriage was just the nudge he needed to break the cycle. It was time to do something or, as Lars said, "risk becoming one more statistic, another failed marriage."

Lars brainstormed. He came up with a list of possibilities. And from that list, he picked something he could do right away to foster more connection and intimacy with his wife, even if he was dog tired. His step was small, but it turned out to have a huge impact.

Each evening, as they both plopped down on the couch, Lars offered to rub his wife's feet. This was something he used to do earlier in their marriage, and he knew she enjoyed it. Even though his "dog-tired" mind said, "You're too tired to do anything," he did it anyway. This small gesture left Lars feeling more connected to his wife.

The benefits didn't stop there. Instead of looking at the TV, they were looking at each other. Instead of falling asleep, they were chatting during the massage. And after just three evenings, they both felt more connected, emotionally and physically.

There was little doubt in Lars's mind that he was doing something good for his marriage, and Annie felt better about their relationship too. These ripples weren't planned. They just happened after Lars took one simple step. Sometimes we just don't know where a step may lead us, or the reach of the ripples we create when we choose to drop a pebble.

The lesson here is that change takes time, but not as much time as you might think. Small changes can make a big difference. You just need to stay on course and be patient. Give any change you make in your life at least three days to take hold, and then take stock. You may have to tweak this or that, or you may have to adjust your course. But if you persist, the change will become a habit in your life, and a good one too.

The important thing is unwavering consistency for three days—no bending, no giving up, and no giving in.

Everything Has a Purpose

When you look back on your life up to now, it may seem that you've lived through a series of haphazard events, without rhyme or reason, some painful, others pleasant—that is, until you stop to notice the strands connecting everything. If you do that, you may find purpose in your joys and in your pains.

You don't have to buy into the idea of fate or predestination to see the purpose in your life. Or you may believe in fate or the idea that everything happens to you for a reason. Be careful, though. Fate can easily turn into fatalism or thinking that you have no role to play—that you're just a pawn, being knocked around by circumstance. This isn't helpful.

Finding purpose in your joys and in your hardships and struggles is a powerful way to add meaning to your life. There are countless examples of people doing exactly that. Consider Pia Pearce and her husband, Simon. They have four boys. The second-youngest, David, has Down syndrome, and the youngest, Kevin, a world-class snowboarder, aspired to compete in the 2010 Olympic Games. Kevin shared a special relationship with David, a relationship marked over the years by kindness and patience. Kevin's gentleness and caring was appreciated, but more so when it was suddenly taken away.

Kevin, one of the world's top half-pipe riders, was just one week out from competing for a spot on the 2010 U.S. Olympic team. Then Pia got a call from the coach. His words were brief and stark: "Kevin's been in a terrible accident. It's bad. You'd better get down here fast."

Kevin hit his head in a bad fall and suffered a traumatic brain injury. The injury left him in a coma and on a feeding tube. He remained in that vegetative state for weeks. Doctors weren't sure he'd ever regain consciousness. And even if he did, hope for any kind of recovery seemed bleak. It was that bad.

But Kevin eventually emerged out of the darkness. First a movement, and then garbled sounds. As we write this, he's still on the path toward recovery and has a long way to go. And as you read this, you might be thinking, how awful, terrible, and sad this is. It is. But there's more going on here than a tragedy, a lost dream, and a damaged son.

This experience changed Pia, Simon, and their family. In a television interview, Pia spoke about Kevin's recovery and said, "I can honestly tell you I feel like there have been miracles unfolding before my eyes, and I am just in awe of having that experience." This tragic experience left Pia more humbled, and with a deep sense of awe and appreciation. And as she looked back, she saw a purpose, the strands holding it all together. This brought her back to the challenges of raising a child with special needs.

She realized that one of the great gifts of David in her life was to prepare her for the trials she faced after Kevin's injury. Pia felt so much better equipped to deal with Kevin's accident because she had David in her life. David had taught her patience, love, and strength. And now David was keeping a watchful, patient, and loving eye over his dear brother Kevin.

The message here is timeless. Life gives us challenges and pain to prepare us for what may come. It can make us stronger, wiser, more patient when patience is called for, or more loving when love is needed. These lessons strengthen us to persist when we might give up, lose all hope, or turn away.

But we have to look for the strands pulling it all together—those threads of values and life purpose. We have to see that everything we've been given has a purpose and can be put to use for good purposes. Even pain can teach us something, alerting us to what truly matters in our lives.

You can look back yourself. What have you lived through that was painful or difficult? If you're struggling now, see if you can imagine that this experience is there for a reason. Perhaps it too has a purpose. What did it teach you? You may not know what that is yet, and that's okay. Just have a look. Imagine that what you've experienced is there to alert you to something right now. Or imagine that it's there to ready you for something later on. It might even be a wake-up call or the nudge you need to break out of a rut and start living your life.

So remind yourself that everything has a purpose, and seek to find that purpose. If you do, you'll find meaning in your life. If you don't, life is likely to seem like a series of unfortunate events, without rhyme or reason.

What Matters Most?

When you look back on your life, you'll find things you wish you had done differently. Our minds love these moments because they're great fodder for regret, shame, and guilt. But there's another way to look at this.

Suppose the past just is. It's a compilation of moments—moments of both wholeness and darkness. And suppose the regret about what happened before is a signal, a harbinger of what matters to you. There's no reason to feel regret or guilt about anything unless you care enough to hurt about it in the first place.

There's no escaping it. When you look back or forward, you'll find your pain, and in that pain you'll find your values. You'll also find your values in moments of utter beauty and sweetness. You have to look for both. What you find might surprise you. And it just might help you as you go forward with the rest of your life—on purpose, with meaning.

We'll end with two simple reflections. Both will help you contact what matters and point you to things you can do—and do now—to live your life on purpose.

Sinking into a Dark Spot

Close your eyes and take an inventory of your life up to the present. Bring your awareness to one painful memory that is seared in your mind. Focus on a memory that still leaves you with feelings of regret, shame, guilt, or brokenness. Look at what happened. What did you do or fail to do in the situation? Jot down a phrase or sentence to encapsulate that memory. Also write a brief statement to describe the situation.

As you sit with the memory, identify the feelings linked with it and label them as you've done before ("I'm having the feeling of..."). Write all of this down.

Now look at what you wrote and take some time with the memory you wrote about. Ask yourself this: If you had it to do all over again, what would you do differently in that situation? Be specific. Write it down. Here's one entry from Beth, a single mom, to get you going.

What I did: *Spanked my three-year-old.*

Situation: *I'd had a long day at work, and he wasn't listening to me.*

Feeling: *Guilt.*

What I wish I'd done differently: *Quietly redirect him, even if he protested. Or make a request, then give him a warning about a consequence, like if he still didn't listen, I'd take away something he likes for a while—a toy or TV time. I'd speak calmly and firmly as I tell him that his behavior is not okay and that I still love him.*

You'll find your values in what you wish you'd done. That's why the memory hurts now. It hurts because the situation was important then, and somehow you failed to act on your values. Or perhaps circumstances, life, or other people conspired against your best efforts. When you allow that history to work against you now, standing as barriers in your life, you'll continue to suffer now.

You can't apply this approach to all painful memories. Sometimes events conspire against you and there is literally nothing you could have done to affect the outcome. Still, your painful feelings about these memories can point you in the direction of your values. This was the case for Jeremy, a Marine captain with two tours of duty in Iraq under his belt. He suffered the scars of war and was haunted with unshakable guilt. His unit was ambushed during a resupply mission. He watched an armored Humvee full of his buddies take a rocket.

Jeremy's training kicked in. He sped up to the burning vehicle ready to help. But all he found was the skeleton of a vehicle and the charred remains of his friends. There was nothing he could do for them. He and they were cheated by circumstance.

His guilt was about this very issue. He was robbed of an opportunity to act on a central value in combat: protecting his buddies and watching their backs, and rescuing them if it came to that. In the years after this gut-wrenching experience, his guilt kept him isolated and alone and continued to rob him of fresh possibilities, like creating new friendships and bonds or reaching out to look after the relationships he still has.

But as he called on his courage to go back to his memories and truly review that day, he saw that there was no way he could have prevented what happened or changed the outcome. The guilt had something to teach him, but to see it, he needed to focus on the value, not just the guilt. He needed to be willing to feel the loss of his friends and be willing to risk loss again.

As he edged himself into that dark spot from his past, he rediscovered something precious. He found that he really cared about his friends and honoring his closest bonds. That's something he'd missed since returning home.

He turned up his willingness and made a commitment to honor his lost friends by honoring his life. He did that by deciding to use his time and energy as best he could. Without retreat or surrender, he took steps to act on his core values about relationships on purpose and with steadfast resolve. He started his days with an intention to turn each "would have done" into "I will do." This led Jeremy to take specific steps to move out of his isolation and into activities and experiences that involved connection with friends and family each day.

Right now, you can do what Jeremy did. Thoughts and feelings about everything you could have done differently may be keeping you stalled out and stuck in pain now, but all of those feelings point directly to your values. If you get specific about what you wish you had done, you'll end up with actions that can bring your intentions to life. You'll end up with things you may be able to do at *this very moment*, and in many ways, to support your values.

You can repeat either version of this exercise with the same memory or new memories. With time, it can help you gain a keen insight into what matters to you and what you can do right now to move forward in your life.

Sinking into a Sweet Moment

Once again, close your eyes and take a life inventory. This time, look for a memory that leaves you with a sense of sweetness and goodness. Maybe it was a birthday celebration or a trip. Perhaps it was a friendship or your first love. Or maybe it was a graduation, a promotion, a new experience, a game or toy, a challenge, or a gift. Whatever you find, just linger with one bright memory that leaves you feeling whole, complete, and good. Sink into it.

Look at what happened during that moment. What did you do? As you notice, label each feeling that comes up. Link it with the sweet moment, with both the situation and something you did. Write all of this down, just as you did before.

Now look at what you wrote. You'll find your values in what you *did* do during past moments of sweetness. That's why it feels good when you remember it now. The good feeling is a gentle reminder that you were in alignment with your values, doing something vital. It just feels right and good to remember that.

And that sweetness may have been hard to achieve. You may have faced challenges back then. But face them you did, and the memory is all the more precious because of it.

It wasn't easy for Mark to find a sweet spot in his life. Shortly after he turned thirty-five, he was diagnosed with multiple sclerosis, an incurable neurological condition. Like Jeremy, he was a victim of circumstance, in this case a disease that ravaged him at the prime of his life. He'd been watching his body and mind slowly deteriorate even since.

That deterioration was hard to take. He couldn't run, he couldn't drive, and he couldn't work like he used to. There were days when he couldn't see clearly, and times when he couldn't see at all. He struggled with fatigue and dizziness, and he had difficulty walking on his own. He also struggled with painful muscle spasms, numbness, and bouts of depression. His mind was slowly slipping away, leaving him forgetful and feeling scatterbrained. Like a thief in the night, these changes crept up on him just as he was hitting his stride.

But it wasn't always like this. Mark closed his eyes and took a slow, deep breath, and then he reflected on the sweet moments in his life. It took a while. But as he relaxed and opened to the experience, in his heart and mind's eye, he found an image of helping his daughter learn how to dribble a basketball. And he lingered with images of how they used to goof around together playing one-on-one games in the town park.

Thinking about those moments left Mark feeling good, and he realized how much he missed that playtime with her. He wasn't able to dribble, run around, and shoot hoops like he used to. But he still had that spirit of playfulness in him. Connecting with this sweet moment made him acutely aware of that.

Mark got out a pad of paper and started making a list. At the top he wrote the word "Play." And then he thought and brainstormed new possibilities with his daughter and his life in mind. He focused on how he could get the spirit of playfulness back into his life, even with his disease.

As it turned out, his list was long. He could swim. He could coach his daughter's basketball team. He could play cards. He even thought of taking a hot air balloon ride with his daughter on her sixteenth birthday. There was more, too. As he put his mind to it and thought outside the box, he realized that the possibilities were almost endless. And the benefits went further. Touching the sweetness of play in his life reminded him that he had a lot of life left to live. His disease couldn't take that away from him unless he let it.

So in both darkness and light, we find our values. When you feel stalled out, you can use these imagery exercises to remind yourself of what you need to do to get back on track and move forward for the rest of your days. Do more of what you wish you had done. And do more of whatever you did that brought sweetness and vitality into your life. That's using your past wisely. That's how you create a life on purpose.

Your Life on Purpose

Let's end our journey where we began, with three questions. You may notice that these questions are a bit different than those we started with. Give yourself a few moments with each one before you read on.

Do I know what matters to me?

Am I willing to face the barriers?

Am I living my life on purpose?

The answer to the last question depends on how you answer the first two. If you say yes to the first question, then you have a clear sense of your values and life purpose—those golden threads interwoven through your life, holding it all together. But knowing that won't be enough. Without willingness to face the barriers—the pain and difficulty along the way—you won't live your life. You'll end up stuck.

If you say yes to willingness, then you're off to a good start. It means that you're willing to take difficult experiences with you as you travel on your way. But willingness won't be enough. Without a purpose, a direction, and concrete actions to take you there, willingness can quickly slide into hopeless passivity. Life ends up being one painful blow after the next, without anything to dignify the pain. That isn't good.

To travel in whatever directions you choose and to dignify the pain of life, you need to link knowing what matters, willingness, and action. Everything in this book has been about helping you forge these connections, for without them, you won't be able to answer the last question, let alone act on it.

So are you living your life on purpose? If that's hard to answer, we'll give you another way to look at it. Suppose we told you that you have twenty-four hours left on this planet. And suppose you could do anything you wish in that time. Anything.

And suppose we told you that what you do during those twenty-four hours will be the only thing you'll be remembered for. How you

207

spend your last day will appear on all of the major networks, in local and national papers, and all over the Internet. Hollywood producers plan to make a movie about your last day too.

This thought experiment isn't about notoriety or doing the right thing for others. It's to get you thinking about transparency in terms of your life. Everyone will know how you lived by what you did on your last day, and you will too.

Take a moment and think about that. Think hard. What would you do? How would you live during those twenty-four hours? Would go to your grave drunk or stoned? Would you die in your office chair? Would you grab something that's not yours, an object or a life, and leave the world a thief or a murderer? Would you spend it harboring bitterness or expressing rage? Would you go out curled up under the sheets or locked in your closet? Remember, you can do anything—no limits. You can pull an all-nighter too.

Look at what you came up with. Most people would fill that day, maximizing every moment, not chasing meaningless tokens. We bet you'd do that, too, if you were given that choice. But here's the deal: You do have that choice. You have it right now.

You are the new day. Each day you're given another opportunity to maximize your time. One day lived that way morphs into two days, then two weeks, two years, a decade, and (we hope) much longer. You just don't know when it will end or how.

You don't know whether you'll be alive to see tomorrow—to listen to music, a sweet voice, a friend's laughter, or the birds singing in springtime. You don't know if you'll be able to walk tomorrow, run on the sand, hug a friend, climb a mountain, or make love to your partner. And you don't know if you'll be able to recognize your lifelong friends, your lover, or your children tomorrow, or even an hour from now. You just don't know. Nobody knows.

What you do know is this: Someday all of it will end. That's a guarantee. And there's something else you know. You know what you have right now, and now is where you act to make a life. How you act is no accident. Accidents happen to us, without our consent. Living your life isn't like that. How you live and whether you do what matters, living out your values, is no accident.

Only you can make it happen. You have a role to play, a say in what you do with your time and energy. You can choose to live your life as if it were happening to you, or you can create a life worthy of your time. One is a life of happenstance, the other a life lived on purpose. It isn't something you can put off until tomorrow. Tomorrow may never come. You only have right now.

Every single creature on this planet will do whatever it can to stay alive. As far as we know, human beings are the only species that's aware that someday it will all end. We know our time is limited, finite. That awareness is powerful. We can use our time well or squander it. Life can be vital, or just about survival. The answer rests in your heart. It's fashioned with your hands. It's expressed with your words. And it's manifested in the direction your feet travel. The proof is in the doing.

You have everything you need to go forward. Your life can be a wild ride, full of awe, wonderment, and appreciation, or you can exit this earth with "it might have been." The choice is clear. The answer rests with you.

Matthew McKay, Ph.D., is a professor at the Wright Institute in Berkeley, CA. He has authored and coauthored numerous books, including *The Relaxation and Stress Reduction Workbook, Self-Esteem, Thoughts and Feelings, When Anger Hurts*, and *ACT on Life Not on Anger*. His books have sold over three million copies. In private practice, he specializes in the cognitive behavioral treatment of anxiety and depression.

John P. Forsyth, Ph.D., is a scientist, writer, professor of psychology, and director of the Anxiety Disorders Research Program at the University at Albany, SUNY. He is an internationally recognized leader in the growth of newer acceptance and mindfulness-based behavior therapies and has won numerous awards for his research and teaching. Forsyth is author of several popular books, including *The Mindfulness and Acceptance Workbook for Anxiety* and *ACT on Life Not on Anger*, and travels widely giving talks and trainings to those interested in learning how to move with the inevitable pains of life and do what matters to them.

Georg H. Eifert, Ph.D., is a psychology professor and Associate Dean of Health and Life Sciences at Chapman University in Orange County, CA. He was ranked as one of the top thirty researchers in behavior analysis and therapy and has authored over one hundred publications on psychological causes and treatments of emotional suffering. He is a clinical fellow of the Behavior Therapy and Research Society and a licensed clinical psychologist. He is author of numerous books, including *The Mindfulness and Acceptance Workbook for Anxiety*.

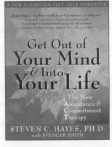